RONA MUNRO

Rona Munro has written for stage, radio, television and film since 1982. Her recent stage credits include *Bold Girls* for 7:84 Scotland and subsequently Hampstead Theatre (Evening Standard Most Promising Playwright Award 1991) and *Your Turn to Clean the Stair* for the Traverse Theatre, Edinburgh (1992). *The Maiden Stone* was the winner of the first Peggy Ramsay Award and was presented by Hampstead Theatre in 1995.

Her television play *Men of the Month*, directed by Jean Stewart, was shown on BBC 2 in 1994, and her first feature film *Ladybird, Ladybird*, directed by Ken Loach was also released that year.

Rona was born and brought up in North East Scotland and writes for the Aberdonian feminist comedy act *The Misfits*.

RONA MUNRO

YOUR TURN TO CLEAN THE STAIR

&

FUGUE

NICK HERN BOOKS
London

A **Nick Hern Book**

Your Turn to Clean the Stair and *Fugue* first published in
Great Britain in 1995 as a paperback original by Nick Hern
Books, 14 Larden Road, London W3 7ST

Front cover: from photograph by Alan Forbes

Typeset by Country Setting, Woodchurch, Kent TN26 3TB
Printed by Athenaeum Press Ltd, Gateshead, Tyne & Wear

A CIP catalogue record for this book is available
from the British Library

ISBN 1 85459 248 3

Contents

Author's Note

Fugue and *Your Turn to Clean the Stair* were both commissioned by the Traverse Theatre, Edinburgh. *Fugue* was the first play I ever had professionally produced and performed. *Your Turn to Clean the Stair* was the last play to be performed in the original Traverse Theatre in the Grassmarket before the theatre flitted to Cambridge Street.

Fugue is not a play I can assess now, it seems kind of strange and raw looking back at it. There are lines in it that make me wince and elements that surprise me with their originality. I was 22 when I wrote it and nearly passing out with excitement all through rehearsals. It was a very happy first experience and it's lovely to see the play in print again. *Your Turn to Clean the Stair* was intended very much as an 'Edinburgh' play. The title refers to the printed notice that is hung on each doorknob in turn as the residents of Edinburgh tenements pass on the obligation to swab down the common stair. Tenement life in Edinburgh creates a particular kind of relationship with your neighbours. Tenements are usually nineteenth-century buildings with three storeys and three flats on each floor. The common stair is the meeting point and its maintenance can become a point of tension. I wanted to write something particular to Edinburgh and I wanted to write a kind of murder mystery. *Your Turn to Clean the Stair* is the result. None of the characters are thumbnail sketches of my neighbours but I was once responsible for losing the all-important notice.

YOUR TURN TO CLEAN THE STAIR

For Barbara and for Gwen

Your Turn to Clean the Stair was first performed at the Traverse Theatre, Edinburgh, on 4 April 1992 and subsequently on tour. The cast was as follows:

LISA	Janet Dye
BRIAN	John Ramage
KAY	Louise Ironside
BOBBY	Graham de Banzie
MRS MACKIE	Kay Gallie

Directed by John Mitchell

Decor by Karen Tennent

Lighting by Tracey Smith

4

Characters

LISA – *Early thirties*

BRIAN – *Early thirties*

KAY – *Early twenties*

BOBBY– *Late twenties*

MRS MACKIE – *Late sixties, early seventies*

ACT ONE

A tenement stairs. We are seeing the middle flight and landing, the stairs continue into darkness above and below. A functioning door opens onto a room in one of the flats. This room is the interior of all the flats we see into, set dressing or backdrops or similar are used to change it from one to the other. When it is LISA and BRIAN's flat the door opening onto the stair is the front door. When it is KAY's or MRS MACKIE's flats the front door is reached through an interior door. There is another door on the other side of the stair, this opens onto BOBBY's flat, the interior is never visible. Other doors are positioned non naturalistically around the set, these open during LISA's dream scenes.

Every time someone enters from the bottom of the stairs we should hear the door bang.

LISA and BRIAN's flat is modern, immaculate and undergoing a constant process of redecoration. KAY's is shabby but full of plants, MRS MACKIE's is also spotless but hasn't been redecorated since 1954.

It is dark. The stair is lit by the light that spills out from the flat doors, they are half open.

LISA is coming down the stairs, slowly, zombie walking, staring front. She is wearing a heavy coat but her legs and feet are bare. She pauses, still staring straight ahead.

Lights and whispering from behind the doors.

Fade lights.

The sound of scrubbing in the darkness. Lights up.

It is early evening. Mrs Mackie is laboriously cleaning the stair. She has two buckets. In one is a scrubbing brush and soapy water, in the other a mop and clean water; this second bucket waits for her at the bottom of the flight of stairs, the soapy one is pulled with her as she crawls down the stairs, step by step, scrubbing slowly and thoroughly into every crevice. She breathes heavily and asthmatically and moves in a way

*that suggests the stiffness in her legs but she can heave her
bucket around with relative ease, she's had a lot of practice.*

KAY *enters, coming up the stairs with a shopping bag, a big
bag of disposables and her baby. Her ascent is almost as slow
as Mrs Mackie's descent.*

KAY. Mind your back, Mrs Mackie.

MRS MACKIE *straightens up to watch* KAY*'s progress.*

MRS MACKIE. You watch your step now, it's slippy.

KAY. I'm going to be putting footprints on your clean stair.

MRS MACKIE. Footprints are the least of this. I wouldn't like
to tell you what I lifted off this stair. I would not.

KAY. It's the dirty weather isn't it?

MRS MACKIE. It's the dirty brute below me. I wouldny mind
but it's no my turn. It's his turn. Two weeks that notice has
been flapping off his doorknob and him paying it no more
heed than the letter box. Well I says we canny be living in a
sewer can we? *Someone*'s got to keep the standards up.

KAY. You're doing a great job, Mrs Mackie.

MRS MACKIE. I'm no wanting thanks. Someone's got to keep
things decent. Engine oil and chip papers and God knows
what, it's all his mess and he just lets it lie.

BRIAN *exits from his flat door carrying a package from
B. and Q. He smiles vaguely at* MRS MACKIE.

What about that front door then son? Will you be fixing
that?

BRIAN *pauses looking at her blankly.*

BRIAN. The front door?

MRS MACKIE. I says to your wife there I says, get that man of
yours to fix that front door so it doesn't bang the wall like
that. Shakes the whole stair. I canny sleep all night with it
banging, that drunken so and so down there in and out with
allsorts banging chunks out the plaster and her up there letting that wee bairn scream it's wee throat hoarse, I says to
her, 'You'll have the social work onto you' she says, 'It's
her teeth.' I says, 'Well you do that poor bairn a kindness,

put a wee drop o' warm whiskey in its bottle and maybe
we'll all get some peace. She says, 'I'm feeding it mysel',
I says, 'Well no wonder it's hungry, no wonder it's screaming, you get that wee girl a bottle.' Young Mums. Starving
their own bairns out of ignorance, I've seen her feed it in
broad daylight too, out on that backgreen, blouse open for
all the world to see, I says, 'This isny the Third World
lassie, you do up those buttons . . .'

BRIAN. It's a problem with the electrics.

MRS MACKIE. It's a problem with standards, you'd never
have seen a lassie carry on like that in my day . . . well no on
this stair you wouldn't, I'm no talking about what you
might've seen down Leith docks . . .

BRIAN. I'd have to take the stair lighting out for a while you
see, the cable goes right behind the hinge there.

MRS MACKIE. Eh?

BRIAN. To fix the door.

MRS MACKIE. It needs fixed, that should've been done long
since, every day that's no fixed I lose another night's sleep.

BRIAN (*vague*). Ah.

    KAY *runs down during this, a frantic dash to collect the
    buggy, her speed increases as the baby starts crying upstairs.*

MRS MACKIE. If I've another night like last night my
nerves'll snap like rubber bands I'm telling you, that noisy
so and so and his pals. They're turning this stair into a
saloon bar. Hoodlums and hoors, well that's what I'd call
any lassie that had herself done up like the wee bit that was
hanging on his arm this last Friday, skirt that wouldn't have
covered a thrupenny bit. Never saw such a thing. Well did
you ever see the like of that?

    KAY *pelting back up.*

BRIAN. Of what?

MRS MACKIE. Of that dirty so and so!

BRIAN. Are you talking about Bobby McNulty?

MRS MACKIE. And what are you going to do about it, son,
that's what I'm asking?

BRIAN. Well . . . I can't say he's bothered me *personally* . . .

MRS MACKIE. About the *door!*

BRIAN. Oh . . . I'll fix it. Yes. Quite simple job really, just need some wood screws. (*Looks at his package.*) I could get wood screws just now I suppose.

MRS MACKIE. And where's the notice? What's he done with our notice? Flapping off his doorknob for two and a half weeks and what has he done with it now? We won't know whether we're coming or going, we won't know who's to do what. That's council property that notice, I could get him fined, arrested . . .

BRIAN. Shouldn't take long. No I could do that. I could fix it now. I'll fix it now.

LISA *enters, climbing the stairs, loaded with shopping bags.*

LISA. Hi, Evening Mrs Mackie.

BRIAN. You're home!

LISA. Yes Brian, I'm home.

BRIAN. It's after five!

LISA. Yes dear, it's five forty-five.

BRIAN. My varnish will be dry!

BRIAN *vanishes back into the flat. He is visible in the front room working on the skirting boards.*

LISA (*calls after him*). Brian, could you give me a hand with . . . oh . . . forget it. That's your shopping, Mrs Mackie, do you want it in your flat?

MRS MACKIE. Oh. Oh I wasn't wanting any messages the day.

LISA. I was just in the supermarket . . .

MRS MACKIE. I wasny wanting anything till Friday. It'll be Friday before I get my pension.

LISA (*bright artificial smile*). I'm terribly sorry Mrs Mackie, I can't go on Friday, I'm going out.

MRS MACKIE. Well I can't buy anything till Friday, I'd enough in to last me till then you see, even saved a jam sponge in case my sister comes round Thursday and I've fish for tonight and one of those Lean Cuisine what-have-you's for tomorrow so I wasn't wanting anything you see. I've all my food in.

A large dog starts barking out back.

BRIAN *sticks his head out the door, waving a paint brush.*

LISA. Look . . . I'll just leave this at your door, it'll not spoil.

BRIAN. Solvent. Did you get solvent?

MRS MACKIE. Oh that's an awfy smell!

LISA. NO!

BRIAN *shakes his head and vanishes.*

MRS MACKIE. I can't be paying you till Friday. I've all my food in you see and I don't get my pension till Friday.

LISA. It's alright.

LISA *moves past her.*

MRS MACKIE. That's how I asked you to get my messages on Fridays you see, 'cause that's when I've the money. That fruit'll be past its best before I'm ready to eat it. Oh that's a terrible smell, you shouldny let him on the stair with chemicals . . .

LISA. Keep the fruit in your fridge.

Dog barking.

MRS MACKIE. You canny put apples in your fridge! I like a fresh apple, they bruise just sitting in the bag. They'll be mush before I get my teeth in them.

LISA. Well I'm *very* sorry Mrs Mackie but I'm on a tight schedule this week, I just had to get it today.

MRS MACKIE. Oh dinny think I'm no grateful lassie, 'cause I am, but I've all my food in you see and I canny pay you till Friday.

LISA. It's alright!

MRS MACKIE. Now are you going to get that man of yours to fix that door? It was banging all hours last night, that dirty so and so letting his pals in to pee up the entry, well someone's daein it, that's all I'm saying though it might be that dog, that great black brute messing our backgreen, have you seen it? Mess, you're no safe putting your washing down for a second. And who's dog is it? Nae collar, it's fat enough though, someone's feeding it, someone's letting their rubbish lie aboot rotting till the dugs and cats tear intae it and spread it all oer the stair and we ken who that is. If my John could see the state o' his garden. Ten hours a day he worked and still kept those edges straight as skirting boards . . .

LISA *is descending rapidly and re-entering with bags of her own shopping during this.* MRS MACKIE *is now rinsing the soapy steps with her clean water.*

He was a great worker John, he could turn his hand to anything. You should have seen that backgreen when John kept it, snowdrops and primulas and sweet peas and roses . . .

LISA. Yes, you said.

MRS MACKIE. He had parsley and rhubarb and grass you could've carpeted your house with, all green, no daisies.

LISA (*smiling through gritted teeth now*). That's right you told me, Mrs Mackie.

MRS MACKIE. Oh he was good, he could fix anything. So are you going to get that man of yours to fix our door?

LISA. I've told him. I'll tell him again. See you later Mrs Mackie.

LISA *enters her flat.*

MRS MACKIE. Aye well he needs another telling. He needs telling till he stirs himself to do it, that's what you need to be doing with that one lassie 'cause he's away in a world of his own if you ask me, wandering round in a wee cloud o' wood shavings without even the time of day in his head and all the time that dirty so and so is banging that door at three in the morning stinking up the back passage with beer and God knows what and . . .

MRS MACKIE *stops dead as* BOBBY *enters whistling happily. He breaks into song as he sees her, spreading out his arms extravagantly.*

BOBBY. 'Sheeee may be the face I can't forge-e-et.' How's it going, Granny? Here.

BOBBY *bounds up to her.* MRS M *is frozen, dripping mop poised, staring at him.*

Wee pressie for you. See this, (*He waves a bottle at her.*) Mould remover, (*Reads off the label.*) 'This mould remover spray works like magic to remove unsightly mould growth and stains from walls, shower curtains, mats etc. Just follow the simple instructions and say goodbye to old mouldy bits forever.' Thought you might like to spray it around, cheer us all up a bit.

MRS MACKIE *doesn't move. He claps her on the shoulder.*

No offence darling, just a wee joke. That's six ninety-nine in the catalogue you know, four ninety-nine to the people with the contacts and I'm the man to contact and this is a wee gift just for you. (*Offers bottle.*) Go on. (*Reads again.*) 'Dispenser bottle has a handy built-in nylon tufted brush to make it self contained for easy use.' Amazing eh? Years of research gone into this. Environmentally friendly as well, it'll turn your walls green, only joking, go on it's yours.

MRS MACKIE *gathers up her mop and bucket, then she turns on him.*

MRS MACKIE. You'll come to a bad end son. I'm telling you.

She staggers away.

BOBBY. Jeezo! I was just trying to be friendly.

He enters his flat and slams the door.

LISA *and* BRIAN *in are in their flat,* BRIAN *on the floor,* LISA *faffing with carrier bags.*

LISA. I've just about had it with that old bat, I have.

BRIAN *is sanding the skirting boards meticulously.*

BRIAN. Hmmm?

LISA. I never even wanted to get roped in as her messenger girl. I ask her once, *once* if she wants anything from the shop and next thing you know I'm spending every Friday afternoon staggering round Safeways looking for single

Scotch eggs and seedless strawberry jam, 'The wee seeds get under my plate'. I'm not saying what I'd like to shove under her plate but it would definitely come with a detonator attached. They'd no avocados.

BRIAN. Oh dear.

LISA. I was going to make guacamole. We were going to have guacamole, Mexican rice and chilli con carne but they'd no avocados. (*Looks at her shopping consideringly.*) I'll make a curry.

BRIAN. An omelette will do me, or a toastie, give me a cheese toastie.

LISA. I'm making a curry, I've all these spices to use up. Is that the property page? (*Pounces on it.*)

BRIAN. How about a pizza?

LISA. That's never Silverknowes, that's bloody Muirhouse. They've got a nerve. 'Extensive parkland'? Extensive wasteground, wild dog packs, pick your own hypodermics.

BRIAN. My grandad lived off Pennywell Road.

LISA (*hands back the paper*). Your grandad had broken glass on top of his garden wall and a rabid Rottweiler guarding his dustbin.

BRIAN. It was a red setter cross.

LISA. It was trained to go for the throat whatever it was. (*She exits rapidly to the kitchen taking her messages with her, calls from offstage.*) I could just put a pizza in, you have to eat them the first day or the whole thing tastes of damp onion . . . Oh I don't know, it's too much trouble to eat anything at all sometimes. (*Delivers part of this from the doorway,* BRIAN *still hasn't moved.*) I'm *wrecked*, it was the last day of the spring sale, half the women in Edinburgh decided they wanted to come in and change the lingerie they got for Christmas. You'd think if you were sharing the sheets with someone you'd notice what colour knickers they wore. What colour knickers do I wear Brian?

BRIAN. Eh . . .

LISA *produces a silk teddy from her bag and holds it against herself, waits for him to notice.* BRIAN *looks up.*

LISA. So what do you think?

BRIAN. That's quite nice.

LISA. You like it?

BRIAN. Yeah, sure.

LISA. You don't think it's right do you? So I'll look fat, so I'll look like a badly made chocolate éclair. what's a bit of cellulite between husband and wife. Close your eyes and pretend it's meringue.

BRIAN. You're not fat, Lisa.

LISA stares at him for a long minute.

LISA. When are we going to put this flat on the market, Brian? The smell from that brewery is getting worse.

BRIAN. It's only when the wind's in the east.

LISA. We might at least find out what interest there is, what price we'll get, we should at least do that.

BRIAN. Time enough for that.

LISA. Well we'll need to get the flat on the market before the summer, we should try and show it in the spring, when there's just enough light for them to see we've got a view of the park but not enough to notice the public toilet's in the way.

BRIAN. Well . . . it depends when I can get the floors done.

LISA. You're going to sand the floors?

BRIAN. Na, they're totally knackered those boards, far too uneven. No I'll have to lift them all and lay new ones.

LISA. How long is that going to take?

BRIAN. Oh I'll get the heavy stuff done over the summer holiday.

LISA. Brian, this is March.

BRIAN. Aye well you see I'd need two weeks at least, not the sort of job you can do in dribs and drabs. I want it to be right.

LISA stares at him for a minute.

LISA. Right? *Right?* This is Abbeyhill Brian, how many colour supplement features have you seen on second floor flats within walking distance of Easter Road? How many times has Country Life done a full page spread on the designer dwellings that litter Spring Gardens?

BRIAN. I can't leave a job half done can I? We'll have to wait and see how my hand heals . . . You know I keep finding things I can't do. I can't open the Marmite jar, something about the shape of the lid.

LISA. You're my childhood sweetheart Brian, you were supposed to sweep me out of adolescence into a better life or at least a better rateable value and you've moved me four streets.

BRIAN. We both wanted to be by the park. (*Flexing hand.*) I can't do my cockatoo.

LISA. I've told everyone we're moving. I told the neighbours, they'll think we can't agree which way is up.

BRIAN. So why worry about them? See I can do my rabbit (*Makes shadow puppet.*) well anyone can do a rabbit . . . and my wolf howling at the prairie moon . . . (*Another puppet shape.*)

LISA. If they're going to watch every last move through their letter boxes I'd like to show at least a *semblance* of rational behaviour!

BRIAN. . . . but I can't do my cockatoo . . . see? He doesn't have a crest. I could call him a parrot but he looks more like a crow really . . . without his crest . . . it's the staff Easter party soon as well, everyone'll be expecting my shadow puppets . . . I might have to sing or something instead.

LISA *crumples up the property page.*

LISA. I said, I *said* that I *had* to move *now*.

BRIAN. It's a busy time of year though, at the school. See Mr Philips, you know the geography teacher? He sang last year. He sang 'Hey Big Spender' and sat on the physics teacher's lap. Well it got a laugh . . .

LISA. And you said 'Whatever you want'! You said it!

BRIAN. Did I? Well let me just get things finished then we'll see.

LISA. Brian!

BRIAN. What?

LISA. I want to *move*.

BRIAN. You want more light, more space and more storage. I hear you. Don't worry about it.

LISA throws the paper in the bin. She stares at it for a minute then she stares at him. She retrieves the paper and uncrumples it, trying to spread the pages around Brian's feet.

LISA. You're getting sawdust all over the *floor*, Brian.

BRIAN. I'll clean it up, don't worry about it.

LISA. Oh will you? When? When you've already tracked it over every carpet in the house?

BRIAN. When I'm finished. Don't worry about it. You know, Cheryl, that's my physio . . .

LISA. I *know* who she is . . .

BRIAN. She was saying I might never retain the full use of those fingers, not the complete range of movement.

LISA. Is that right.

BRIAN. She said I just ought to be prepared because there's always a delayed reaction with any disability, however minor.

LISA. You're not disabled Brian. If you can hang out the window waving a Black and Decker sander at the woodwork at 8.30 on a Sunday morning you are *not significantly* disabled.

KAY is coming down the stairs.

BRIAN. Not completely.

LISA. More's the pity.

BRIAN. But I am restricted in what I can do. I can't do my cockatoo, Lisa.

Pause.

LISA. Fine. Fine. I'll be in the bathroom cutting my wrists, that O.K. with you? (*Exits at full speed.*)

BRIAN. Lisa? (*Door slams off.*)

Look don't *break* anything; the retiling took . . .

A smash of glass, KAY *rings the doorbell at the same time.* BRIAN *groans then goes to answer it.*

BRIAN. Hullo.

KAY (*looking past him*). Is eh . . . is Lisa in?

BRIAN. She's in the bath.

Another smash of glass.

KAY. Oh . . . well listen, I know it's awfy short notice but I was wondering if she could watch the wee one for me tonight?

BRIAN. Tonight?

KAY. Aye, I was wanting out, just for a quick drink, I've no been out since teeny arrived . . . And then this friend's been asking me for ages . . . anyway Lisa said she might babysit for me sometime ?

BRIAN. Oh that'll be alright.

KAY. You sure?

BRIAN. No problem.

KAY. It's a bit cheeky such short notice.

BRIAN. Don't worry about it.

KAY. Oh that's brilliant, could she . . . well could she make it up in about half an hour?I mean no if she's in the bath or . . .

BRIAN. Half an hour, that'll be fine, I'll tell her.

KAY. Oh that's great! Thanks.

BRIAN. No problem.

KAY (*starting back upstairs*). Oh thanks a million.

BRIAN *closes the door.* LISA *re-enters ostentatiously applying elastoplast to a small cut in her hand.*

LISA. Oh thanks a million Brian!

BRIAN. You didn't damage the tiles did you? Only I had to go all round town to match those.

LISA. Just what I wanted to do tonight, wade in liquid sewage and listen to tiny piercing screams.

BRIAN. You told her you'd baby sit!

LISA. I was only being polite! I mean I bumped into her on the stair when she was waddling up with eight tons of laundry practically dripping milk on every step so what could I do? It was a casual remark! Don't know what she's thinking of taking me up on it. Cheeky? I'll say it's cheeky. That man of hers knew what he was doing, getting out before the nappy buckets started overflowing in every corner.

BRIAN. Lisa, did you break any tiles?

LISA. No. I broke the mirror.

BRIAN. Oh that's alright.

LISA. Is it?

BRIAN. Yeah. I was going to replace that, I fancy putting in three big mirrored cabinets, what do you think? Make a bit more storage space.

LISA holds up her wrist.

LISA. It's a deep cut.

BRIAN looks at her, crosses over and takes her hand, kisses her wrist.

BRIAN. There. All better.

LISA just looks at him.

LISA. Whatever you want.

BRIAN. What?

LISA. Tiles, mirrors, whatever you want.

BRIAN. I'll go and clear up the bathroom.

He exits. LISA stares after him for a moment then exits onto the stair.

Lighting change.

A door half open, light and voice coming from behind it. LISA edges towards it. BOBBY is talking on the phone. MRS MACKIE's voice is descending the stair but she does not become visible.

BOBBY. No listen, she's beautiful, she is . . . stripped down a treat . . . no come on Tommy, we're talking class here, class, you want to see the movement she's got . . . aye . . . aye . . . naw, better than that . . .

MRS MACKIE. Well she's well turned out, I'll say that for her, but she's a sharp tongue in her head.

BOBBY. Two grand, all she needs is a new transmission.

MRS MACKIE. But I'm no one to gossip, aw no, take people as you find them, I wouldny believe a story like that about her, I would not.

BOBBY (*under this*). Aye O.K. Wednesday.

MRS MACKIE's *door bangs upstairs.* BOBBY *exits onto the stair almost cannoning into* LISA *on his step. Lighting change.*

(*Waving mop.*) She's got us all feart eh?

LISA. What?

BOBBY. Time I took a turn, let no-one say I don't take my turn.

LISA. She's just done that.

BOBBY. Eh?

LISA. Mrs Mackie, she's just finished.

BOBBY. She said it was my turn!

LISA. It was. It's been your turn for the last month.

BOBBY. Aw for . . .

LISA. It's O.K. You've no detergent in that bucket anyway have you?

BOBBY. So?

LISA. Nothing.

BOBBY. Look, all you're doing is wetting the bloody things. There's folk walking up and down all day with muck on their shoes for God's sake, they're *stairs*, it's no an operating theatre is it? She'd have me out there shampooing the street.

LISA. She does wash that bit of pavement, that's how our kerb's paler than the rest of the road. She leans out the window and screams at the dogs when they go in our gutter.

BOBBY. She's got a problem, I'm telling you. Jeezo, went and bought a bloody mop as well. It's a good mop but. Handle collapses, head comes off so you can fit a duster on, do your pelmets. £12.99. You could have this one for seven pounds dead, it's only damp.

LISA. Since when did you dust your pelmets ?

BOBBY. I've no pelmets darlin, I've no curtains. I've nothing to hide.

They look at each other for a minute.

I've no seen you.

LISA. No.

BOBBY. Where are you off to the night?

LISA. I'm babysitting for Kay up the stairs. She's going out for a drink.

BOBBY (*laughs*). Oh aye, I know what pub that'll be.

LISA. What?

BOBBY. Nothing. So how've you been?

LISA. I'm fine thank you. How are you?

BOBBY. I'm getting on, you know. Just closed a wee deal the other night there so that's me in the money.

LISA. Good.

BOBBY. Thought I might celebrate.

LISA. Yeah, you should.

BOBBY. Wee night on the town.

LISA. Well . . . enjoy yourself. (*Starts to go upstairs.*)

BOBBY. So eh . . . listen . . .

LISA *stops.*

BOBBY. You're looking great, by the way.

LISA *just looks at him. He puts the mop down, takes a few steps up to her.*

You are. You're looking great.

LISA *doesn't move.*

What've you got on?

LISA. What does it look like?

BOBBY. Naw . . . underneath.

LISA (*sweet*). You want to know what colour knickers I have on Bobby?

BOBBY (*smiles*). Aye.

LISA. Why don't you dive back down the sewer you crawled out of eh? And take your expanding mop with you.

She runs up the stairs leaving him staring after her, stunned. KAY looks up as she hears the bell, goes to let LISA in through internal door. BOBBY steps back and knocks over his bucket.

BOBBY (*roar*). Aw SHITE!

KAY (*ushering LISA in*). This is dead nice of you.

LISA (*bright smile*). Oh it's no trouble,

KAY. Really, you're saving my life.

BOBBY contemplates the water flowing down the stairs then he kicks the pail.

What's the racket?

LISA. Bobby McNulty.

BOBBY snatches up pail and mop and exits into his flat, slamming the door.

God, he gives me the crawls, he does.

KAY. Bobby's alright.

LISA. I should never have told him I managed lingerie, it's like telling him I run Fantasy Island.

KAY. Does he bother you?

LISA. Oh aye.

KAY. Bobby? Really? He hassles you?

LISA. Oh aye.

KAY. He's never bothered me.

LISA. Well he wouldn't, would he?

KAY. How?

LISA. You're a mother!

KAY. Oh aye . . . right.

LISA. God . . . (*Shivers.*) Can I smoke?

KAY. Aye, just sit by the window.

LISA *looks out as she lights up.*

LISA. There's that dog.

KAY. The black one? I hate that dog.

LISA. It's got a bone the size of Portobello.

KAY. It was on the backgreen the other day, who'd let it onto the backgreen? I'm feart to leave Tina out in her pram.

LISA. It can jump the wall from the park.

KAY. It's no a dog at all. It came out a zoo that thing.

LISA. She won't wake up will she?

KAY. No, she doesn't usually, just sing to her if she does.

LISA. *Sing* to her?

KAY. Aye, anything'll do. She quite likes Madonna.

LISA. I don't need to pick her up or anything do I?

KAY. Not if you don't want to.

LISA. I just . . . well you know, she wouldn't be used to me.

KAY. She won't wake up, don't worry. This is really nice of you.

LISA. It's alright.

KAY. Does the place look O.K?

LISA. Sorry?

KAY. Well you've just come in right? So you're seeing it fresh. Does it look alright?

LISA (*uncertain*). Aye . . . it's fine.

KAY. But does it look like I'm on top of things?

LISA. Your baby's asleep, you've made your own bread and there's no dust on the skirting boards. I'd say you had things under control.

KAY. Aw brilliant. Sorry for asking, you know, but I'm that nervous.

LISA. You got someone coming round?

KAY. Aye.

LISA. Oh?

KAY *puts bread in tins, offers nothing further.*

So do you still hear from Dave?

KAY. He's in Falkirk.

LISA. Oh? Living with . . . em?

KAY. Aye, he moved in with her.

LISA. And has he not even seen the baby?

KAY. No.

LISA (*clicks her tongue*). Well you need cheering up eh?

KAY. It's a woman.

LISA. Sorry?

KAY. It's a woman I've got coming round.

LISA. Oh?

KAY. My social worker.

LISA. Oh I see. I didn't know you needed . . . I mean that you had eh . . .

KAY. I thought the whole stair knew.

LISA. Well you can't believe gossip can you? (*Awkward pause.*) Well you really need cheering up then don't you?

LISA *rummages in her bag and produces a silk teddy with a flourish.*

Ta ra! Now don't worry, it was in the sale and I got staff discount so it hardly cost me the price of a drink.

KAY. What is it?

LISA. What does it look like! Now trust me, Kay, I've seen this a million times. If you get this on you you'll not just sing like Madonna you'll *feel* like Madonna. Try it, go on. (*She pushes the teddy at* KAY.) Mind you she's a sight isn't she? I mean I don't think that's dancing, that's just showing yourself off.

KAY. I don't think it's me.

LISA. Well of *course* it isn't. That's the *point*. You see you've got to understand the psychology of this, Kay. Look at you. You look like a wee china doll, a tiny pure and perfect bit of Victorian porcelain and you're wearing *black silk*. Their neanderthal brains will just explode.

KAY. Whose?

LISA. Men! Believe me, I know what I'm talking about. You think it's obvious, you think it's crude but they will go for it *every* time. I can wrap Brian round my little finger. How do you think I get so much home decorating done? Put on one of those and say 'Brian we need to sand the floorboards' and before you know it we're living in Homes and Gardens. I can get anything I want out of him.

KAY. I don't think I'd feel comfortable.

LISA. But it *is* comfortable. (*Pushing it against* KAY *again.*) It's so soft you don't know it's on. *Feel* it.

KAY (*offering it back to her*). It's just not my style.

LISA. Oh well, I was only trying to help.

KAY. I know. Thanks, I mean, sorry.

LISA. You see you may think that's . . . vulgar or something but it works. You have to try what works. The Bobby McNulty's of this world trip over their own tongues at the sight of something like that. (*Shudders*.) Oh, he really upsets me.

KAY *is putting the bread in tins, covers it with a cloth.*

KAY. You should tell him if he's bothering you. You can talk straight to Bobby. He's O.K.

LISA. Oh you think so do you? Well . . . He was making funny remarks about you, I have to tell you.

LISA *starts picking things up off the table, looking at them, examining* KAY*'s walls.*

KAY. What?

LISA. I said you were going out and he says 'Oh aye, I know what pub that'll be.' Very knowing look.

KAY looks at her for a minute but doesn't say anything.

Probably got you doing go-go in his head, slimy wee perve. How do you grow so many *plants?* I can't grow mould on cheese.

KAY *(wiping her hands)*. I'll need to get away. My friends are waiting.

LISA *(picks up seed packets)*. What are these?

KAY. I'm going to brighten up that back green. Wee bit of colour for Tina to see in the spring.

LISA. Have you told Mrs Mackie?

KAY. No.

LISA. You're just going to dig up her garden!?

KAY. It's no hers.

KAY gets her jacket, purse.

LISA. So how would Bobby know what pub you're going to?

KAY. Oh they let anyone in. I'll put the soup off now. Help yourself while it's hot though.

LISA. Bobby just likes to sound as if he knows it all.

KAY. Bobby's just got a big mouth. See you later.

Exits.

Lighting change. One of the doors opens a crack, a voice whispers up the stair.

VOICE. Lisa . . . Lisa.

LISA *seems to be dozing, she looks up. She slowly opens the door and looks down the stairwell. All the doors on the stair slowly open. Light and voices come from behind them.*

VOICE. Lisa?

VOICE. Oh she doesn't fool anyone. Tripping around in those smart wee suits like she's never even thought about taking her shoes off . . .

VOICE. What are you wearing Lisa?

VOICE. Under your coat Lisa?

VOICE. Up and down with her nose in the air, like she'd only lift her skirt to straighten the hem, like she's sewed into her stockings. We've seen her type on this stair afore this, she's no fooling *anyone*.

VOICE. What are you wearing, Lisa?

VOICE. Tell us, Lisa.

VOICE. Show us, Lisa.

LISA. It wasn't me!

LISA *runs back into the flat, slamming the door. There is a sudden thunderous knocking. Lights up as* LISA *hits the table, scattering its contents.* MRS MACKIE *is hammering on* BOBBY*'s door.*

MRS MACKIE. Where's our notice you dirty pig! You pass that notice out to me right now!

LISA *gives a quick nervous glance towards where the baby is sleeping then goes out onto the stair.*

I know you're in there! I can hear you! All hours of the night I can hear you! You can turn that telly down while you're about it!

LISA (*hissing*). Mrs Mackie! Mrs *Mackie!* You'll wake the baby.

MRS MACKIE (*turns*). He's got the notice! He's never passed it on. It's a council notice. 'It is your turn to wash and sweep the common stair'. Well who's to know who's turn it is now? It'll stay his turn till judgement day now, won't it? 'Cause he's sitting on the notice. It'll be his turn till the roof drops in now but no-one'll ever do it but me!

LISA. Look I'll do it next week, alright?

MRS MACKIE. It's no your turn! If it's no his turn it's them across the landing! But it is his turn! It'll never get past his turn till he washes the stairs and passes on the notice!

LISA. He did them tonight, O.K?

MRS MACKIE. What!

LISA. Mrs Mackie, can you keep it down, the baby's not long asleep and . . .

MRS MACKIE. But I did them tonight.

LISA. He did them after. He's an ignorant pig, Mrs Mackie, don't bother about him.

MRS MACKIE. Is he saying I didny do them right when I was up and down with two pails of water and it wasn't even my turn!?

LISA. He never noticed what state they were in. Look . . .

MRS MACKIE. I should get the council onto him.

LISA. You should. I would.

MRS MACKIE. Sitting there in all his stoor with jungle music coming up through my floorboards. Well I'm telling you, I've had it. This was a decent stair . . .

LISA (*interrupts*) Well why don't you sort him out, Mrs Mackie someone should.

MRS MACKIE. Then Mr Murray at the bottom died and poor Ina went into the home and nice Mrs MacPherson with the wee scottie that never went in the street . . .

LISA. You get the council onto him Mrs Mackie, then you'll sleep easy.

MRS MACKIE. Oh someone should sort him. If my John was here he'd've had words , he would. He had the whole stair spotless, anyone missed their turn he just had a wee word, that's all it took, he had that back green just immaculate, that's all his flowers out there, primulas and snowdrops and roses, that's still his roses . . .

LISA. Beautiful roses, it's a shame to dig them up.

Pause. MRS MACKIE *stops dead mid flow and gapes at her.*

Oh it's just what I heard, It's a common green of course so technically we can't stop anyone planting any sort of weed, nasturtiums, dandelions . . . whatever . . .

Still nothing.

They could drive a mechanical digger right through your lovely garden and all we could do is shake a tea towel at them.

MRS MACKIE (*croak*). What?

LISA. But *not cleaning* the *common stair*. Well you could get the council to take some notice of that couldn't you?

MRS MACKIE. Who's digging up my garden?

LISA. Bobby. Bobby McNulty. Bobby is going to dig up your garden, Mrs Mackie. Bobby McNulty is going to stick a shovel right into your rose bed.

MRS MACKIE. That's my John's garden. He never let anyone touch that but him.

LISA. I know.

MRS MACKIE. No-one's touched that garden since he went.

LISA. I know, but Bobby's not going to bother about your feelings is he? He'll be right in there with a spade and a cut-price rake. You should get the Council onto him Mrs Mackie, I mean you're the one knows what this place used to be like, *ought* to be like. You could sort him out.

MRS MACKIE *walks past her, still silent.*

Someone should see to him.

MRS MACKIE. That's my John's garden.

LISA. I know. You'll need to stop him.

MRS MACKIE. Oh. Oh I haven't the strength for this I haven't.

LISA. Mrs Mackie . . .

MRS MACKIE. Oh John, I've no the strength left for all this . . .

Exits.

BOBBY*'s door opens slowly. He peers round it at LISA.*

BOBBY (*loud whisper*). Is she away?

LISA *just looks at him.*

You saved my life again darlin, thank you. Tell you she had me just about crapping mysel there, sounded like ten guys wi' hammers for hands trying to get in. I'm a wee bit jumpy just now you know. Floating a bit of finance. Thought I'd got mysel a bit of bother on the doormat there.

LISA *holds the stony stare for a moment then turns to walk upstairs.*

Oh! Hold on a minute!

She turns back.

What did I do? Come on, just tell me, O.K? What did I do?

Still nothing.

I thought we were getting on great. You even gave us a Christmas card! So what was that about?

LISA. It's a long time since Christmas, Bobby.

She walks away from him.

BOBBY. Aye, you're right there.

BOBBY *slams his door.*

LISA *enters* KAY's *flat from the internal door, sees the scattered seeds and starts to clear up agitatedly.* KAY *is slowly climbing the stairs.* LISA *is left with handfuls of seeds and bread with no bag to put them in. She looks round, startled as* KAY *comes in.* KAY *stops and stares.*

LISA. Sorry, I knocked them over.

KAY. What are you doing?

LISA. I was just . . .

KAY. Get out of my stuff!

LISA. But . . .

KAY. Get out of my stuff!

LISA *steps back as* KAY *dives in and starts sweeping everything into her arms.*

There was a letter here! Where's the letter!?

LISA (*faint*). It's over there. (*Points.*)

KAY *snatches it up, examines its contents swiftly as if checking to see if it has been read. Her shoulders slump.*

KAY. Shite.

LISA. I was sleep walking I was just . . .

KAY *looks at her.*

I fell asleep and then there was banging on the stair and I knocked into everything . . .

KAY. Right.

LISA. I mean I'm sorry . . .

KAY. Is Tina O.K?

LISA. She was fine.

KAY. Great. (*Slowly puts things away.*) I don't like folk touching my stuff.

LISA. Well I didn't go through your drawers, Kay!

KAY. Oh I'm sorry I . . .

LISA. I mean I can't help it, it's a tension thing.

KAY. I'm just a bit upset.

LISA. It's actually very common. One in five people sleep walk at some point in their lives. It doesn't mean they're *disturbed* or anything.

KAY. No, I didn't mean . . .

LISA. You've got a dead leaf sticking out of your pocket.

KAY. It's not dead. (*Pulls it out.*) It's an ivy cutting. It was a present.

LISA. Oh?

KAY. Goodbye present.

LISA. Well you better plant it.

KAY. No I'll not bother. It is nearly dead. (*Drops it on the table.*) Thanks for baby sitting.

LISA (*gathering up bag*). That's alright. Just give us a bit more warning another time, O.K?

KAY. Yes of course, it was really good of you . . .

LISA. I need to have a few days' notice, I do work you know.

KAY. Yes.

LISA. Well, I'll get away.

KAY. Right, goodnight, thanks, really.

LISA. Night.

> LISA *exits.* KAY *clears the room of her stuff.*

> *Lighting change. Whispering from behind the doors.* LISA *walks slowly downstairs. She pauses outside* BOBBY'*s door for a long moment as if about to knock.*

> *The doors open again. Light and voices from behind them,*

VOICE. It's alright, Lisa.

VOICE. Just show us.

VOICE. Tell us.

VOICE. What have you got on?

VOICE. Well you can tell, can't you? You can tell just by looking at them. Oh yes, it's written all over them. Never lays a finger on her. Oh you can tell. Well would you?

VOICE. Show us, Lisa.

VOICE. Oh she'd have you think it's the perfect marriage, but she's not fooling anyone. He can't stand to touch her. Well would you?

VOICE. Tell us, Lisa.

VOICE. Oh she can polish all she likes but she can't put a shine on that. She's not fit to be touched.

VOICE. What's under your coat Lisa?

LISA. *Nothing!*

VOICE. Well you can hear everything through these walls. She can't keep secrets here. Poor man canny move for the rolling pin on his back.

VOICE. Lisa . . .

VOICE. It's my belief they've only done it twice in the last six months. Twice. That's all. You can see it in her face, her tight polite smile. She can't hide a thing, it's leaking out the seams of her little black suit, her underwear's whispering it into the air as it flaps all clean and fresh and limp on the line. They *don't do it at all!* Well would you?

LISA. Shut up!

VOICE. Oh she's a desperate woman. Can't hide that.

LISA. SHUT UP! JUST SHUT UP!

Blackout. There is a death rattle type groan in the dark.

Lights up. LISA is awake and staring at BOBBY who is sprawled at her feet. He has a hole in the back of his head. There is blood. LISA looks. After a minute she moves stiffly to crouch beside him and feel for a pulse. She checks his wrist and then his neck. She stands up again. She doesn't move again for several moments. There is the sound of heavy breathing and a clanking bucket. MRS MACKIE begins to descend behind her. LISA whirls round and runs up to her. They stop, nose to nose. LISA is blocking MRS MACKIE from seeing BOBBY.

LISA. Mrs Mackie.

MRS MACKIE. You'll catch your death.

LISA. What?

MRS MACKIE. You ought to get some slippers on your feet. I'm needing past, lassie.

LISA. What are you doing?

MRS MACKIE. He's made a terrible mess of the stair, it's aye his turn but he just lets it lie and . . .

LISA. You've done it.

MRS MACKIE. Eh?

LISA. You washed the stair earlier tonight and he took his turn after, remember?

MRS MACKIE. I *know*, I'm no daft am I? I need to do it again.

LISA. No.

MRS MACKIE. Eh?

LISA. Why? Why do you need to do it again? It's fine.

MRS MACKIE. I heard him, did you no hear him?

LISA. No.

MRS MACKIE. There'll be some mess down there, I'm telling you. Leave it to tomorrow it'll be dried in. We'll never lift it.

LISA. What?

MRS MACKIE. Him! Dirty drunken so and so, puking his fish suppers all over my clean steps! Did you not hear him?

LISA. No . . . No it's . . . it's clean Mrs Mackie. I've just come past his door, it's clean.

MRS MACKIE. I heard him.

LISA. It's all clean.

MRS MACKIE. Well . . . I'll have a look in the morning and I'm telling you now, if I find what I think I'll find I'll be at your door with the bucket and the mop and *you* can sort it out.

MRS MACKIE *starts to climb slowly again.* LISA *turns back to* BOBBY, *approaches him slowly. Obviously nothing has changed. She wheels abruptly and runs into her flat.*

LISA. Brian!

She waits for a response then runs into the other room.

LISA (*off*). Brian!

LISA *re-enters and walks slowly towards the outer door again. As she approaches it all the lights go out.* LISA *gasps with fright in the dark. The outer door bangs heavily. There are the sounds of heavy feet coming up the stairs.*

LISA. BRIAN! BRIAN!

The feet start to run. The light goes on in the room. BRIAN *is standing at the door with his hand on the switch.*

BRIAN. What is it? What's happened?

LISA *can't speak. He crosses to her quickly.*

BRIAN. You've been sleep walking? It's O.K., it's O.K. Lisa you've just been walking again . . . come on now, deep breaths . . . deep breaths . . . you're breathing too quick Lisa, slow it down, that's it . . . you're O.K. love, you're O.K. I've got you . . . I've got you . . . it's alright . . .

LISA *slowly gets herself under control. She hugs him. He strokes her head.*

LISA. I killed him.

BRIAN. What?

LISA. I was asleep. I was sleep walking. I don't *know* what happened. I keep sleep walking, Brian. I keep getting the dream. I think . . . I think . . . I killed him! I killed him. You know what I'm like . . . I had the dream again I . . .

BRIAN. Who's dead?

LISA. Bobby, Bobby McNulty!

BRIAN. There's no-one out there.

LISA. He's there! Didn't you see?

BRIAN. I was fixing the door, I've cut the light cable, I was just coming up to get some spare wire.

LISA *turns to listen to noises from the stairwell.*

LISA. There's someone out there! I can hear them! There's someone out there!

BRIAN. Look you've been having nightmares again, that's all.

BRIAN *disentangles himself and takes tools and wire out of his toolbox.*

Just sit down, concentrate on your breathing, I'll fix the lights and then you'll see everything's O.K.

LISA. Don't leave me! Don't leave me alone, Brian!

BRIAN. It's alright, I'll only be a minute.

He dashes out and down the stairs. LISA sits trying to breathe deeply for a minute, then she gets up and walks towards the door, peering out. The lights come on. The landing is empty. LISA stares for a moment, then goes to touch where his body was. Her hand comes up bloody. She crouches, looking at it, looking round. She rubs her hand on her arm, sees the blood on herself. She gives a low whimper and runs back into the flat, into the inner room. BRIAN is coming up the stairs. He gives a quick look round the landing then enters the flat.

Lisa?

She appears at the inner door, scrubbing her hands with a damp cloth.

LISA. His blood's on me! I've got his blood on me!

BRIAN. Lisa, come out here.

He leads her out into the room.

Come and look, there's nothing there.

LISA. No.

BRIAN. There's no-one there.

LISA. He's gone.

BRIAN. There wasn't anyone there.

LISA *looks at him for a long moment.*

LISA (*quiet*). I wasn't dreaming. Bobby was there. He was dead. He was bleeding. He's gone. (*She waits.*) You don't believe me.

BRIAN. There's no-one there, Lisa.

LISA. I know. But he was. And he was bleeding. He had a hole in the back of his head, there's blood all over the landing.

BRIAN. No there isn't.

LISA*'s face crumples.*

LISA. Oh I *want* it to be a dream, I *want* it to be a dream but it *wasn't!*

BRIAN. Yes it was.

MRS MACKIE *is meanwhile coming down the stairs with her bucket. She puts it down, tuts at the state of the floor and starts swabbing. BRIAN and LISA talk over this.*

LISA. I know what a dream feels like. I was awake.

BRIAN. Come on pet, why would you have killed anyone?

LISA. Oh Brian . . . Oh God, Brian, you know what I'm like.

Pause.

BRIAN. That's just stupid.

LISA. No.

BRIAN. *Yes!* (*Quieter.*) Yes it is. I've told you this, listen to me, you had a nightmare, O.K? That's all.

Pause.

LISA. Why were you fixing the door in the middle of the night?

BRIAN. I couldn't sleep. Anyway, it was the best time.

LISA. For what?

BRIAN. To take the lights out.

LISA. I'm not strong enough. I'm not strong enough to do that. Smash someone's head in. You'd have to be big wouldn't you? Someone bigger, someone stronger . . . it *must've* been . . . mustn't it?

BRIAN. Lisa, this is all in your head.

LISA. You didn't like him . . .

BRIAN. He didn't bother me.

LISA. What do you mean he didn't bother you? You don't care! Is that what you're telling me?

BRIAN. Well what are you saying, Lisa! Are you saying I hit him over the head with a hammer!?

LISA (*quiet*) . . . . No.

BRIAN. No. Because no-one did. You imagined it. You *dreamt* it, Lisa.

LISA (*shaky*). But Christmas . . . at Christmas . . . you . . .

BRIAN (*cuts her off*). NO! (*Pause.*) I'll get you a drink.

Exits through flat.

LISA *hears the sound of mopping outside. She goes to look.* MRS MACKIE *looks up at her.*

MRS MACKIE. What did I tell you? Filthy brute.

LISA. What . . . what was it?

MRS MACKIE. Eh?

LISA. On the floor . . . what was it?

MRS MACKIE. His mess! That's what! I told you, his mess everywhere just like it always is.

She picks up the bucket and mop.

MRS MACKIE. It's you should've been cleaning that up, lassie. It's you.

She turns and walks upstairs with her load. LISA *watches her go.* BRIAN *comes back and hands her a glass, his voice is controlled.*

BRIAN. We're not going to talk about Christmas, there's no need to talk about Christmas. Is there? You should just forget it, that's what's giving you nightmares.

BRIAN *exits.*

Fade lights. In the dark the sound of Bruce Springsteen's version of 'Santa Claus is coming to Town' played from inside BOBBY's *flat on a ghetto blaster, loudly.* BOBBY *joins in, erratically, the sound of hammering.*

Lights up. BOBBY *is nailing a large and very tacky Xmas garland onto his door, Bambis and tubby Santas.* MRS MACKIE *enters at the top of the stair and stands staring down at him. He turns and sees her, jumps.*

BOBBY. God almighty. I never heard you.

MRS MACKIE. Well you wouldny would you?

BOBBY. So how's it going?

Nothing but a baleful stare.

BOBBY. Cold eh? Freezing. Brilliant eh? . . . Well maybe no . . . you feeling it? Feeling the cold?

Still nothing.

BOBBY. Listen, I've got the very thing, just got them in, electric socks, battery operated, completely safe, 'less you wear them in the bath. £5.99 two pairs for a tenner what do you reckon?

MRS MACKIE. Do you know what time it is?

BOBBY. Aye it's about ten thirty . . . Oh . . . (*Realisation.*) Sorry.

BOBBY *ducks back into his flat, turns off Bruce Springsteen. Comes out on the stair.*

BOBBY. O.K? Sorry about that.

MRS MACKIE *starts to walk upstairs again.*

BOBBY. So what about the socks? £4.99 two pairs for £8, what do you say?

MRS MACKIE *doesn't turn.* BOBBY *resumes hammering and singing loudly. She turns then and stares, then resumes her climb, muttering.*

MRS MACKIE. My John would've sorted you, oh aye, he would, sorted you quick enough.

The door bangs below, then KAY *enters, climbing slowly. She is heavily pregnant.* BOBBY *stops hammering.*

BOBBY. Are you no away yet?

KAY *shakes her head, breathless.*

BOBBY. Hang on a minute, will you.

He runs down and takes her arm, helps her up the stairs.

BOBBY. You sure it knows the way out?

KAY *shakes her head.*

BOBBY. Aye, knows where it's well off that's for sure. Do you want to stop, have a wee seat?

KAY. If I sit down, I'll no get up.

BOBBY. Have a rest though, I'll get you a drink eh? Wee Christmas drink . . . Oh Christ you canny though eh?

KAY. What've you got?

BOBBY. Champagne.

KAY. You're kidding.

BOBBY. I'm no.

KAY. That'll do.

BOBBY *hands her the bottle, turns to get mug,* KAY *has already taken a swig from the bottle.*

KAY. Oh . . . Oh that's horrible but I like it. I can feel the bubbles.

BOBBY. That'll maybe shift him.

KAY. Her.

BOBBY kneels and shouts at the bump.

BOBBY. Do you feel that wee one? Do you? That'll get you jumping. Come on. Come out and see Santa. (*He looks up at her.*) Dave coming home for Christmas?

KAY. No.

BOBBY. But he'll be back for the wain?

KAY. No.

BOBBY. Shite . . . What'll you do?

KAY (*shrugs*). Cope. Maybe.

BOBBY. But . . .

KAY. I've got friends, Bobby.

BOBBY. Oh.

He gets up.

KAY. What?

BOBBY. Nothing. You've got friends. Great.

KAY. Aye, it is.

BOBBY. If you're sure they're good for you, friends like that.

KAY. Like what?

BOBBY. It's your life.

KAY (*very hard*). Bobby, are you going to mind your own business?

BOBBY. Always do.

KAY. You better.

BOBBY. Look I'm just thinking of the bairn, right? It just . . .

The door bangs below. They both turn to look.

KAY. I'm warning you Bobby, you keep your mouth zipped, hear me?

She attacks the remaining stairs with the best turn of speed she can manage as LISA appears below. LISA looks up.

LISA. Oh . . . Hi. (*Calls.*) Hi Kay.

KAY (*calls back without turning*). Hiya.

    LISA *leans on the bannister and looks at* BOBBY.

BOBBY. Aye aye.

LISA. Aye aye yourself.

BOBBY. Bit of festive spirit?

LISA. More than a bit. Works outing, two drinks and we were all screaming like hyenas. It's fatigue. It's been Looney tunes' time on our floor. Christmas stampede. Every bum in Edinburgh must be wearing black lace and silk if we've had anything to do with it.

BOBBY. Oh very nice.

LISA. Aye, you wouldny think it to look at half of them would you? Here . . . (*Rummages in her bag.*) This is yours. (*Holds out a card.*)

BOBBY. What's that?

LISA. A hand grenade, what does it look like? Christmas card.

BOBBY. God's sake.

LISA. What?

BOBBY. No-one sends me these, bar my mother.

LISA. Well I'm in good company amn't I?

BOBBY. I wouldny say that.

LISA. We give one to every flat.

BOBBY. Right.

    LISA *hesitates a minute.*

LISA. Well . . . Happy Christmas. (*Moves towards her door.*)

BOBBY. Eh . . . listen . . .

LISA. What?

BOBBY. Don't fancy another wee celebration do you? I've a couple of bottles of fizzy stuff.

LISA. What've you been up to. Launching ships?

BOBBY. Christmas sales, I'm winning, I'm telling you, I'm hitting oil.

LISA. Good for you.

BOBBY. Want to see? Come on in, I'll show the whole range, give it your professional opinion.

LISA. I think I need to get home.

BOBBY. O.K. O.K. Just wait there then . . .

BOBBY *grabs mug and fills it swiftly. Hands it to her.*

LISA. Listen I've really had enough . . .

BOBBY. Back in a minute.

He dives into his flat. LISA *shakes her head, smiling, sits down on the steps and takes a swig of champagne.* BOBBY *reappears with several packages.*

BOBBY. Right. This is gold this, canny get enough of them. (*Hands her package.*)

LISA (*looks*). It's a pig.

BOBBY. It's a *diet* pig. You're after that extra helping of trifle right? Open the fridge door and it oinks at you.

LISA. It *whats* at you?

BOBBY. Oinks, you know . . . (*Makes pig noise.*)

LISA *collapses.*

BOBBY. What? (*Laughing.*) What? They're mugging me to get these I'm telling you. Then there's this . . . (*Holds it up.*) The Bonny babe drinks dispenser, see the wee boy on the top there right, fill up the bottle, press the button . . . you watching? This is artistic this . . . there you go, he pees in your drink for you.

LISA. Oh. Oh that is gross!

BOBBY. Listen there's Greek statues that areny as artistic as this . . . now this is a real seller, combined, torch, hoover and neck massager, want to try?

LISA. No! Bobby, how do you make a living?

BOBBY. I'm fighting them off, I'm telling you.

LISA. Where do you get this stuff?

BOBBY. Different suppliers . . . you know.

LISA. I don't think I want to.

BOBBY. Oh nothing too dodgy. It's getting the capital together that's dodgy, always seem to find myself talking to guys in suits that bulge where they shouldny and deliver payment reminders through your door with their boots.

LISA. So what happened to the profits from the last lot of mega sales?

BOBBY. Spent! God knows where. Aye well, life's too short for savings accounts eh? (*He refills their mugs.*) Don't know where it all goes. I was married once, you know? Don't know where she went to either. (*Looks at her.*) Only joking. Here's to you. (*Drinks.*) Nice to get to know you, by the way.

LISA. What?

BOBBY. No-one talks, do they? You could bleed to death on this stair and all they'd do is tell you to mop it up. Woman at the bottom shakes every time I come near her, only asked if I could get her bag for her, that old battleaxe up there on at me to clean everything in sight and you've never given me much more than a wee hullo with frost on it.

LISA. Well . . . That's how it is isn't it?

BOBBY. How?

LISA. You're all on top of folk on a common stair, you need to keep a bit of privacy.

BOBBY. What for?

LISA. Well . . .

BOBBY. Och no listen, forget it, just nice to get to know you. Here's to you. (*Drinks again.*) So.

LISA. So.

BOBBY. Here we are.

LISA. Yes.

They look at each other.

BOBBY. Happy Christmas.

LISA. Happy Christmas.

He reaches out and just touches her. LISA freezes.

I better get in.

She puts her mug down.

BOBBY. O.K. Right. Sorry. I'm sorry, O.K.

LISA. What?

BOBBY. I'm sorry.

LISA. What?

BOBBY. I got the wrong end of the stick . . . I thought you . . . just imagining things, bubbles in my brain . . . sorry.

LISA *waits.*

BOBBY. Just you look so fucking gorgeous, you know? No offence right? Sorry.

Pause.

LISA. Say that again.

BOBBY. God how many . . . I'm *sorry* . . .

LISA. *No.* What you said . . . how I look.

BOBBY. You look great. You always do. I could just . . . Never see you except in that coat but . . . Always wondering what's underneath.

LISA *slowly takes off her coat, watching him the whole time, she's wearing a Christmasy dress underneath.*

LISA (*quiet*). It's no that exciting, it's just a dress.

BOBBY. It's beautiful.

Pause.

They kiss, then LISA tries to stop.

LISA. No . . . *No!* . . . Not here. Not here.

She gets up and moves quickly into his flat. BOBBY follows. LISA's coat lies abandoned on the steps.

Lighting change, doors opening and whispering from behind them, time has passed.

BRIAN *comes into the flat room looking rumpled and sleepy, wearing night clothes. He puts on the light, looks at his watch, frowns.*

LISA *emerges from* BOBBY's *flat, closes the door, tries to do it quietly but it bangs.* BRIAN *opens the door onto the stair.*

LISA *stares at him for a minute then walks quickly past him and off through the room.* BRIAN *is left looking at her coat on the stair. He walks over and picks it up.* BOBBY's *door opens and a half-dressed* BOBBY *sticks his head out.*

BOBBY. Oh listen . . .

BOBBY *stops, blinks at* BRIAN *for a minute.*

BOBBY. Aw . . . Eh . . . Merry Christmas.

BOBBY *closes his door.* BRIAN *doesn't move.*

Fade lights.

End of Act One.

ACT TWO

The sound of someone knocking on a door.

Lights up. LISA *is standing on the landing in her dressing gown. She has just knocked on* BOBBY'*s door. She waits and knocks again.* MRS MACKIE *appears at the bend in the stair above her.*

MRS MACKIE. Pssst!

    LISA *looks round, startled.*

    Come up here will you, I'm needing a word.

LISA (*weary*). I'm off sick, Mrs Mackie.

MRS MACKIE. I'll no keep you.

LISA. I'm not dressed.

MRS MACKIE. It's three in the afternoon, it's time you were. Come on, I've the fire on.

    LISA *climbs wearily up as* MRS MACKIE *enters the room through the inner door. This is now her flat, old furniture and a beeswax shine on everything including the upholstery. She fidgets a few cushions then calls through as she hears* LISA *outside.*

MRS MACKIE. Come away in, close that door behind you.

    LISA *enters.* MRS MACKIE *peers at her.*

    You been drinking?

LISA. I've been ill. I've not slept.

MRS MACKIE (*snorts*). Well . . . Sit yourself down. I've tea made here.

    Tea, cups and biscuits are sitting out in good, old china. MRS MACKIE *busies herself in pouring as* LISA *watches, bemused.*

MRS MACKIE. Sugar?

LISA. What?

MRS MACKIE. Do you want sugar?

LISA. Oh . . . no . . . thanks.

MRS MACKIE *hands her the cup.*

MRS MACKIE. You'll take a biscuit though.

LISA. No . . . I . . .

MRS MACKIE *thrusts the plate at her, commanding.*

MRS MACKIE. Go on, they're Garibaldi biscuits, take two.

LISA. One's fine, thanks.

MRS MACKIE. I like a Garibaldi biscuit. That was John's favourite too, every night half eight sharp, cup of tea and a Garibaldi biscuit. Oh there was all sorts of bother if I'd none in, he liked his routine. Half eight cup of tea, nine o'clock bed. Every night the same. He needed his sleep he said, for the morning, for his work. I'd maybe want to finish some chores, get the floors done while his boots were out of my road but that wouldny do, oh no, nine o'clock he was to be in bed and me in with him, that's how he liked it. Routine.

LISA. Yes.

MRS MACKIE. He liked his routine. He'd his own mind just how things should be so that's how they were you see.

LISA. Yes.

MRS MACKIE. Oh aye.

MRS MACKIE *stares into space reflectively for a minute,* LISA *just sits, nursing her cup.*

Strong willed you see, he was strong willed, well he was a strong man, you wouldny have thought it to look at him but he was. Oh aye, he'd some power in his arm. You see what I'm saying?

LISA. I don't know.

MRS MACKIE *stares at her for a minute.*

MRS MACKIE. Garibaldi biscuits. You know the last person that sat in that chair and supped my tea, apart from my sister that is, but I wouldny get the good china out for her, the last person I had in here wouldny touch them. Health visitor or something, I put them all out and she never even sniffed at them, on a diet or some nonsense. Well I've no money to waste on biscuits have I? You'd think she would've seen that. This was last March when I'd that bother with my sciatica, never got it sorted yet, you think she'd've taken a bite of biscuit, just for hospitality wouldn't you?

LISA. Yes . . . (*Takes a reluctant bite of biscuit.*)

MRS MACKIE (*chewing as well*). They've lasted well though. Kept well in the tin.

LISA *looks at her biscuit with sudden distaste.*

Maybe a wee bit soft. John couldn't stand a soft biscuit. Oh no, these wouldn't have done for him, theyd've been in the fire and the plate after them. Oh but he was a quiet man, that's what everyone said, he was, a quiet man, he never had to raise his voice. (*Takes another bite.*) See, long as I'm left in peace in my own house I'm fine, there's enough to do keeping things straight, running a kitchen, I'd no microwave, oh no, I made my own bread, no-one else on the stair was up to that, I made sponge cakes you could've tied a string on and given the bairns for a balloon they were that light, he knew he'd got a good cook when he got me. See I had my routine and he had his, just as long as we stuck to that, that was alright. I'd the cleanest step on the stair. (*Another bite.*) Half eight tea and biscuits, nine o'clock bed every night . . . you've something to put up with when you get married, well you'll know all about that.

LISA. What?

MRS MACKIE. You're married.

LISA. Yes.

MRS MACKIE. It's the quiet ones that're the worst.

LISA. You said you wanted a word?

MRS MACKIE *appears to focus on her again. She gets up, pulls out some photographs.*

MRS MACKIE. That's John . . . see? And that's my Jean and my Robin. Jean's in Canada, Robin's in Australia, they take after him you see, he was aye hankering to emigrate. Went and got us papers and everything, I'd never been further

than Portobello beach, Leith was as foreign a place as I ever
wanted to see, there were some queer folk down in Leith
then, believe you me. Oh, but he was all for a new life on
some prairie somewhere, I says 'Can you imagine the dust
that'll come in off a prairie?' There's nothing to stop it there
is there? It'd just blow for miles. I'd enough bother doing
my corners. Oh but he couldn't see it . . . Anyway he died.
He didny suffer you know, he was always bad with his
heart. It was quick at the end.

LISA *hands back the photos.*

LISA. Mrs Mackie what did you want to see me about?

MRS MACKIE. Well it's him isn't it?

LISA. Who?

MRS MACKIE. Him downstairs.

LISA. Bobby?

MRS MACKIE. You said it yourself, he needs sorted.

LISA. I shouldn't have said some of that, I was just . . .

MRS MACKIE. Oh but you understood, didn't you? I could
tell from what you said, you know what's what. You do . . .
don't you?

LISA (*uncertain*). Yes.

MRS MACKIE. You need peace in your own home don't you?
That's all any of us want, peace in our own homes, you
understand that?

LISA. I suppose.

MRS MACKIE. So.

LISA. What?

MRS MACKIE. Well he's needing shifted isn't he? Off the
stair. We don't want him on the stair. You'll need to see to it
lassie, I've no the strength.

LISA. I don't think . . .

MRS MACKIE. You'll need to sort it out now.

LISA. I'll . . . maybe have a word . . . if I see him.

MRS MACKIE. Oh you'll see him. Canny miss him.

LISA. No.

MRS MACKIE. Well that's good of you, that's a load off my mind. You're always well turned out, I'll say that for you, I thought you'd see what was what.

MRS MACKIE starts to clear up the tea things briskly. Recognising dismissal, LISA gets up slowly.

MRS MACKIE. Oh and could you get me loose tea in my messages next time? I dinny like they tea bags, dust they're filled with. You could get me it in the corner shop today if you like.

LISA. I don't know if I'll be out.

MRS MACKIE. Oh well, when you've time. I'll not be out myself. Don't like that wee shop anyway, they shouldny dress the kids like that, I hate to see that. They should be like us when they come over here and then people would like them more. I says that to her up the stairs and she says 'That's an ignorant way to talk,' the cheek of it! 'That's an ignorant way to talk', that's great coming from her, at least I've the sense I was born with, at least I've kept all my wits between my ears and not sent half of them flying off to the moon. That poor bairn. She's no long out you know.

LISA. Out of where?

MRS MACKIE. The Royal, Psychiatric. Oh she was violent. I heard all sorts of screaming before they lifted her. That poor bairn. They should sterilise them you know, it'd be a kindness in the long run.

MRS MACKIE exits with the tray. LISA follows slowly.

MRS MACKIE (*off*). Close that door behind you.

LISA reappears on the stair, KAY is coming up holding her baby. LISA stops.

KAY. Can I come into your flat. I can't go into my flat.

LISA just stares at her.

I've got to get off the stair. I've got to hide! Please!

LISA steps aside to let her into the flat, follows her in. KAY settles the baby carefully on the sofa then runs back to close the door. Breathing fast. Listening.

KAY. They're outside. Did you see them?

LISA. Who?

KAY. Two of them. Built like transit vans, . . . God. I'm shaking.

LISA. What do they want?

KAY. Bobby! They're his 'business associates'. You must have seen the kind of company he keeps.

LISA. But why would they . . . ?

KAY. Shhh! Is that them? Are they coming up? Oh shite!

LISA. What do they want with you?

KAY. I don't hear anything. Do you? They don't want me, they want Bobby!

LISA. But . . .

KAY. Listen, the last person who saw Bobby McNulty is in big trouble, *big* trouble. They'll want someone to answer for him.

LISA. The police . . . I'll . . .

KAY. NO! (*Quieter.*) No you can't do that. (*Looks at* LISA.) You don't know Bobby that well do you?

LISA. No.

KAY. Well . . . If I say he got what was coming to him you'll just need to take my word for it.

LISA. You . . . don't like him.

KAY. This time he was being really stupid. (*Listens.*) They're no coming in. (*Looks at baby.*) She'd sleep on if a tank came through the wall . . . just as well eh? The bastard, the stupid *bastard*. Oh he's got what was coming to him. (*Looks at* LISA.) I've got the shakes now. I . . . (*Bites her lip.*) I need eh . . . I need to take something . . . I'll need to ask you to get me something. I'm sorry.

LISA. We haven't got anything like that.

KAY. Like what?

LISA. We've only got paracetamol. We haven't got much of that. In fact we probably haven't got any.

KAY *stares at her for a moment.*

KAY. Cup of tea would do. Just as long as it's sweet. I'll make it myself if you like.

LISA. I'm not well. I was just going to lie down.

KAY (*quiet*). I can't go out there yet. I'm sorry but I can't pick up my wee girl and run up the stairs and try and get my door open without dropping her when there's two guys down there all fuelled up and ready to kick the shite out of anything that moves. I can't do that. I have to wait till they're gone. I have to wait till I've stopped shaking. I can't go to pieces just now, she'll need her tea in half an hour.

LISA. I'll put the kettle on. (*Exits.*)

KAY (*calling after her*). I'm sorry to have to ask. I really am, O.K? I'm . . . I'm sorry. (*Walking over to look down at her baby.*) She's only been here seventy days. I've counted them all. Seventy days and no-one's asked for her back yet.

Bobby used to kiss my bump, you know? From the minute I showed. Shouting Hiya through my belly button. Stupid bastard. No-one else wanted her here at all. He used to touch her, tickle her toes through my skin. I should forgive him anything for that, shouldn't I? (*Quieter.*) But I can't.

KAY *looks up as* LISA *comes back in with a mug.*

KAY. We'll be out your road in a minute.

LISA. You've known Bobby a long time.

KAY. Since before we moved on the stair. He sold cars then and bikes. Sold David a 750 that nearly killed him, both wheels exploded first time he took it on the motorway, Bobby probably nicked them off a pram or something. Came to see Dave in the hospital with a six pack and a carry out, curry and charm, conned him out of two hundred for a new set of leathers. Bobby always was trouble . . . What is it?

LISA. What?

KAY. I'm jumpy. Sorry but . . . what you looking at me like that for?

Pause.

LISA *starts to tidy things distractedly.*

LISA. Mrs Mackie's a terrible gossip isn't she. Mind like a doormat. Every bit of grime that's ever been up the stair has stuck in there somewhere. 'Course she exaggerates everything.

KAY. You've been talking to Mrs Mackie?

LISA. She had me in for tea. *Disgusting* tea. Tap water on a tea bag, she's probably saving electricity.

KAY. No-one's been past her step but her sister and the health visitor since 1968.

LISA. Well you wouldn't go twice. Believe me. She'd be better in a home really I think. She can barely manage. I mean I don't *mind* doing her shopping but . . .

KAY. What did she say about me?

LISA. Oh she talks about everyone, it's sad really I mean . . .

KAY (*interrupts again*). Carried off to the loony bin was I? Screaming, strait jacket, mouth full of foam? (*Waits,* LISA *doesn't reply.*) You canny keep secrets on this stair can you, but all Mrs Mackie sees is what she spies through the fish eye on the door.

LISA. Well really it's no stigma *now* is it? I mean . . .

KAY. You want to know her secret? Her and dear departed John? Departed himself all the way to Canada didn't he? Everyone knew. They were still talking about it when I came on the stair and she's giving it 'Poor John and his poor heart,' don't know how she thought she'd pull that off with no funeral. She's the one with real problems, no me.

LISA (*even more frenzied dusting*). Well we've all . . . I mean I'm sure we all *could* be unstable . . . if the circumstances arose . . . I mean I cut up Brian's paint overalls with a pair of scissors once.

KAY. And I cut my wrists with the bread knife.

KAY *holds up her arms, pulling down the sleeves to show the scars, she holds them up for a moment as* LISA *stops dusting and stares.*

She didn't tell you that?

LISA. No.

Pause.

KAY. I'm sorry. You didn't deserve that. I'm sorry. It was Bobby wasn't it?

LISA. What?

KAY. Bobby told you the rest. I knew he had last night. Too late to shut him up. (*Snorts.*) The last person you'd think to see in a dyke bar, Bobby McNulty.

LISA. A . . . dyke bar?

KAY. Trying to flog them Madonna table lamps, can you believe it? You'd think he'd caught me mainlining heroin, the look on his face . . .

Pause.

LISA. I didn't know.

KAY. What?

LISA. I didn't know you were . . .

KAY. Lesbian.

LISA. Yes.

KAY. Oh . . . well I suppose you do now. (*Pause,* KAY *shakes her head.*) Shite . . . Aw shite . . . Dave never knew either. That's no why he left . . . I'd probably have him back you know. You'd do anything for company wouldn't you?

BRIAN *enters at the bottom of the stairs, he walks up to* BOBBY*'s door and bends down, apparently peering through the letter box.*

They say we're not fit to be mothers, don't they? People say that. Mrs Mackie would say that. They'd take Tina away from me. (*Suddenly fierce.*) I'd *kill* before I let anyone take Tina away from me.

BRIAN *suddenly bangs the letter box.* KAY *and* LISA *jump.*

Oh *God* . . . it's them.

BRIAN *bangs it again.* KAY *goes to pick up the baby.*

I can't get past them. I can't . . .

LISA *doesn't say anything.*

You don't want me here.

LISA. I . . . I just need to rest. I'm ill. I'm very . . . Look, just phone the police!

KAY. NO! (*Quieter.*) You mustn't. You just mustn't.

BRIAN *bangs the letter box again.*

Oh the bastard, he brought them here, what was he *thinking* of? Well I'm telling you if there's going to be violence it'll no be me gets damaged this time. No this time, I've damaged mysel enough, it's someone else's turn now. (*Shouting at door.*) You hear me? (*If possible the baby is awake and screaming over this.*) Come near me and see what you'll get!

KAY *dashes at the door and exits onto the stairs starting to run up them. She freezes at the sight of* BRIAN *gaping up at her. She stares at him for a long moment.*

Damp sort of day isn't it?

BRIAN. Terrible.

KAY *walks up the stairs at normal pace as* LISA *comes to the door.*

BRIAN. Is she alright?

LISA (*dead*). I think she's got a therapist as well.

BRIAN *looks back at* BOBBY'*s door.*

BRIAN. See? I thought I'd seen sawdust. It's dry rot. He's got dry rot.

LISA. What are you doing here Brian?

BRIAN. It's my lunch hour, I was finishing the door off. He'll need to see to that Lisa, it'll spread to the whole stair. (*He looks up at her.*) You look terrible.

LISA *says nothing.* BRIAN *comes up to her.*

Have you been in bed?

LISA. No.

BRIAN. You should lie down pet, you're washed out. Come on.

He puts his arm round her, leads her into the flat.

LISA. I'm fine.

BRIAN. Well sit down then, come on, I'll put a cushion at your back. (*Does so.*) Is there anything for a sandwich?

LISA. I don't know.

BRIAN. I'll just grab myself something, don't you worry. (*Moves to inner door.*) Just close your eyes Lisa, you'll feel better. (*Exits.*)

LISA sits. Her eyes stay open but the lights slowly dim. She gets up and walks out onto the stair. She looks at BOBBY's door. It opens. BOBBY comes out. He is bleeding. He stands swaying, looking at her. LISA doesn't move. BOBBY falls to his knees. Slowly the other characters appear on the stair, BRIAN from downstairs, KAY and MRS MACKIE from upstairs, BRIAN is carrying a hammer, MRS MACKIE a mop, KAY a broom. They come to stand on the landing with LISA, looking at BOBBY. BRIAN steps forward and hits BOBBY with the hammer, BOBBY groans and falls forward. MRS MACKIE and KAY join in, laying in with broom and mop. BOBBY collapses and lies still. BRIAN uses his feet and the women the broom and mop to sweep and push him down the stairs. They look at his fallen body and then turn and look at LISA. BRIAN hands her the hammer, exits. She looks down at BOBBY, steps forward, BOBBY is trying to crawl away. The women turn and walk slowly upstairs looking back over their shoulders. BRIAN comes on again, he is wearing a grotesque clown's mask and carrying three juggling balls.

BRIAN. Lisa?

A lighting change. The other characters have gone. LISA is alone on the stair with BRIAN, the hammer in her hand.

Lisa what are you doing?

LISA starts and looks round.

LISA (*uncertain*). Brian?

BRIAN doesn't move, just stands looking at her.

Brian please say something.

BRIAN abruptly starts doing the Looney Tunes theme while attempting to juggle.

BRIAN. Th . . . th . . . that's all folks! (*Pushes up mask.*) What do you think?

LISA *stares.*

It's for the Easter show, do you think the kid's'll like it?

LISA *puts her hands to her face and starts to cry.* BRIAN *moves quickly to her.*

What is it?

LISA. I don't know.

BRIAN. Come into the flat, come on.

He leads her in.

LISA. What are you doing home again anyway? It's the middle of the afternoon.

BRIAN. It's seven o'clock.

Pause.

LISA. It can't be.

BRIAN. Have you been sleep walking again?

LISA. I don't know.

BRIAN. I'll get you a drink.

He takes off his coat, gets her a brandy, talking as he does so.

I don't like seeing you like this.

LISA. Brian, I'm going crazy.

BRIAN. No you're not.

LISA. We've got two options. Either I'm overdue a fitting for the strait jacket or somebody killed Bobby last night and hid the body.

BRIAN. You were *dreaming* . . .

LISA. Someone on this stair. His heavy friends wouldn't be looking for him if they'd wiped him out.

BRIAN. I've got something to show you.

LISA. It was one of us. One of us killed him.

BRIAN. He's not *dead.*

LISA. Then I'm insane.

BRIAN sighs.

BRIAN (*gentle*). Just calm down and listen will you? Drink your brandy. Go on.

She takes a sip.

Now, I know you're upset, but this is how it is, Lisa.

LISA. What?

BRIAN. This is where we're going to be. This is my home. We don't want to move yet. I'm *settled* here, you see? I thought we were happy.

LISA. Happy?

BRIAN. This is what you *wanted.* I've put a lot of work into this place Lisa, to make it right, to make the home we wanted. Look . . . look . . . (*Showing her the room.*) Imagine the floors sanded, nice pale pine glow off the wood, stucco effect on the walls, I'll sponge the paint on, yellows and muted orange right? The walls'll light up, it's going to be *beautiful,* Lisa. You've got to give me time, to get it right . . . look I can build in shelving units, you want more storage space, I can get antique pine and make them to measure. I can *do* it Lisa. This is going to be the home you *want.*

LISA. I wanted it in Marchmont.

BRIAN. I like it here. This is where I'm *settled.*

LISA just looks at him.

I can't win can I? Got to be the way you want, always something more, something bigger something better before I'm half way through giving you what you asked for the first time . . .

LISA. I don't want you to paint the walls Brian, I never wanted any of that.

BRIAN. Well what *do* you want!?

LISA. I want to see someone.

BRIAN. Who?

LISA. A doctor . . . a . . . therapist, someone.

BRIAN. There's nothing wrong with you! You're just depressed.

LISA. I want *us* to see someone.

BRIAN. Why?

LISA. You know why.

BRIAN. Lisa if you don't stop nagging about this it won't get better.

LISA. It isn't getting better Brian, we need *help*.

BRIAN. I don't want to move Lisa and I don't want to go to a doctor. It's no-one else's business.

LISA. Why don't you just say it? You don't want me, I repulse you I . . .

BRIAN. NO!

LISA. Then why won't you touch me!?

BRIAN. I don't want to move flat Lisa and I'm not going to a doctor. What would you say to a doctor?

LISA. That we never make love.

BRIAN. We *do* . . .

LISA. Five times in eighteen months.

BRIAN. So, who's counting?

LISA. *I* am!

BRIAN. I can't sit in front of some doctor and listen to you say that. I won't. It isn't true, it's more complicated than that. We can fix it ourselves.

LISA. We won't!

BRIAN. We will!

LISA. So fix it.

BRIAN. What?

LISA (*quiet*). Come and hold me Brian.

BRIAN. Now?

LISA *nods,* BRIAN *sighs.*

LISA. You see?

BRIAN. Oh God.

Slowly he goes over and holds her awkwardly.

LISA. Kiss me.

BRIAN. Lisa . . .

LISA. Please!

He kisses her, trying to go straight into passion, she starts pushing him away.

NO! That's too rough! Not like that . . .

BRIAN. You see! You see! I'm always wrong! Whatever I do! And you wonder why I won't . . .

LISA. It's Bobby isn't it?

BRIAN. What!?

LISA. You're never going to forgive me for screwing Bobby McNulty.

BRIAN. Oh for God's sake, that isn't important.

LISA. WHAT!? (*Grabs his hand.*)

BRIAN. It's finished with! Stop dragging it up again!

BRIAN *pulls away, clutching his hand, wincing.* LISA *stares at him for a moment.*

LISA. What's wrong pet? Hand still sore? Too much strain on your wee fingers? You shouldn't exert yourself. Got to get your fingers fit. Got to be able to waggle your fingers at the lovely Cheryl eh? Do you talk about it? Your terrible disability? Do you tell her how you got crippled? Are you crying on Cheryl's white antiseptic shoulder and telling her what a poor bruised and battered husband you are?

BRIAN. I told her it was an accident.

LISA (*interrupts*). It *was* an accident. It *was!*

BRIAN. You hit me with a hammer, Lisa!

LISA. I was just wanting to make you stop! Just stop *stroking* and *fondling* the bloody woodwork when I was trying to talk, to *touch* to . . . Well you could see I was upset! You *knew*. Did you want me to hit you? Is that what you wanted, Brian? You made me cry then didn't you? I'd've done anything to say sorry then wouldn't I? You touched me then, you held me then. Is that what I've got to do Brian? Beat some affection out of you?

BRIAN. All I want Lisa, all I want is some peace in my own home!

LISA. You want her? Cheryl? You want to do it with her? Go on, I don't mind, it's alright. How did you put it? It's not important. At least I'd have the satisfaction of knowing you were touching something human instead of making it all with your Black and Decker Workmate!

BRIAN. Just stop this . . .

LISA. No! Go on, go for it, it doesn't matter does it, I screw Bobby, you screw Cheryl . . . oh but you won't will you? Have you told her that? Have you told her that you never do it at all, but it isn't important?

BRIAN. Shut up!

He snatches the hammer off her, holds it half raised.

That's what you want isn't it? You want me sweating and raging with jealousy, you *wanted* me to kill him didn't you?

She doesn't answer, terrified.

See? . . . I do know how to make you really happy, don't I Lisa?

He snatches up his coat and goes to exit.

LISA (*whisper*). I just want you to touch me like he . . .

BRIAN *exits onto the stair, going down.* LISA *watches him go then turns and walks upstairs.*

KAY *enters the room and makes it hers, she's dressed for bed.*

MRS MACKIE *appears at the foot of the stairs, looking up, she calls up.*

MRS MACKIE. That you up there lassie? There's mess down here still needing sorted . . . You hearing me? There's mess down here still needing sorted . . .

A knock on KAY*'s door. She goes to answer it.*

MRS MACKIE *waits for a reply for a minute, then turns and walks down again, muttering.*

I don't know, I've it all to do, I've it all to do.

She exits. LISA *appears at the inner door of* KAY*'s flat.* KAY *follows.*

LISA. Am I disturbing you?

KAY. Och I can stay awake another twenty minutes. I go down about nine these nights, it's the only way to keep your brain in the third dimension.

LISA (*holds up bottle*). Brandy.

KAY. Oh . . . well I don't . . .

LISA *is already pouring drinks.*

Alright . . . just a wee bit . . . Listen . . . I'm sorry, I lost the place a bit today. I've no had much sleep.

LISA. No. No, nor have I.

KAY. He's borrowed thousands you know. And they're on to him this time. They'll get him this time. He's no business bringing trouble like that to my door, no when I've a wee one to worry about. I canny forgive him that.

LISA. No.

KAY. 'Course you don't like him.

LISA. No.

KAY. I couldn't let you get the police in on it Lisa, they might save his life, but if they ever get a look at his books he's dead anyway.

LISA. Is he?

KAY. What?

LISA. Dead.

KAY (*pause, looking wary*). Well . . . I hope not, he owes me a tenner.

LISA *stares at her searchingly, she slowly refills her glass, takes another swig.*

LISA. I . . . I wanted to ask you something.

KAY. What?

LISA. It must be hard.

KAY. What?

LISA. Being . . . like you are.

Pause.

KAY. And what, like is that?

LISA. And with Tina. It must be such a worry, people can be so judgmental and it's instinct isn't it? You're her mother, you'd do anything for her wouldn't you?

KAY. Yes I would.

LISA. It's like a tigress isn't it, or a lioness or . . . humming birds are really aggressive about it, I'm sure I saw that on David Attenborough . . . you'd kill for her, it's instinct.

KAY. Well . . . let's hope it never comes to that.

LISA. People's sex lives are their own business. No good ever came of talking about it. None.

LISA *takes a nervous swig.* KAY *watches her steadily.*

They shouldn't take people's kids. I saw one of those American T.V. movies about it. I was crying so much I dripped all over our Turkish kelim, you're not even supposed to dry clean them, it's got little lumpy bits on it now . . . So I wouldn't tell anyone.

KAY. What?

LISA. That you're . . .

KAY. A lesbian?

LISA. Yes.

KAY (*snorts*). Tell who you like, just don't tell Mrs Mackie, she gives me enough dirty looks as it is.

LISA *freezes, staring at her.*

KAY. Och, sometimes it's easier if folk don't know, sometimes it's easier if they do, I just like to pick that myself as I'll tell

Mr big mouth McNulty next time I see him. (*Laughs.*) Na, I'll probably lend him more money. Och he's stupid but he's been good to us, you know?

LISA. But they'll take Tina . . .

KAY. Who?

LISA. Social workers.

KAY. *Social workers?* You'd need a pretty senseless social worker to try and split up a great wee team like me and teenie.

LISA. What about your social worker?

KAY. God Lisa, whose toothbrush do you think that is in my bathroom? I'll say this for going off your head, you get introduced to a whole new social circle.

LISA *stares at her, then whispers.*

LISA. It wasn't you. (*She drops her head into her hands.*) It wasn't you.

KAY. What?

LISA *starts to cry quietly.*

What is it? (*Goes to hug her.*) Darlin what is it?

LISA. It wasn't a dream. I know what the dreams are like this was . . . It was *real.*

KAY. Shhhh.

LISA. I can't *breathe.*

KAY. Aye you can.

LISA. I can't breathe!

KAY *strokes her back.*

KAY. No you're alright, you're alright pet, it's just panic, we all get it, just slow the breathing down, that's it, you're *fine.*

LISA. I can't stop thinking about it, seeing him lying there . . . thinking about him smiling at me. Smiling at me.

KAY. Who?

LISA. Smiling. I made him smile.

KAY. There you go . . . that's better . . . slow, quiet breathing that's it . . .

LISA. All wrapped up for Christmas, pink camisole and French knickers in washed silk, have you felt that stuff? It's like skin. Black stockings, ten denier, I looked like Royalty with half its clothes on . . . He just stared and stared and smiled like Santa Claus had finally brought him the perfect stocking filler. He *loved* it.

KAY (*surprise*). You love it!

LISA. What?

KAY. All that lingerie stuff, *you* love it don't you?

LISA. So?

KAY (*laughing*). Nothing darling, it's just funny, don't worry about it.

LISA. What have you heard?

KAY. Heard?

LISA. About me?

KAY. Och I never hear anything, I'm never out my door, ken?

LISA. You get out for a wee drink in your club though eh? Girls only?

Pause.

KAY. Aye.

LISA. So you wouldn't be one to judge.

Pause.

KAY. You didny need to say that.

LISA. Aye well. I'm the total bitch, ask Brian.

KAY. I like Brian.

LISA. You can have him.

KAY. You're not happy?

LISA. What's that?

KAY. Why don't you leave?

LISA. Well you can't leave just because you're not *happy* can
you, show me someone happy who hasn't been drawn by
Disney. Anyway I've got my eye on a nice little garden flat
in Trinity and I'd never get the mortgage on my wages,
Brian says for that price we could have ten rooms in
Niddrie, *Niddrie!?* I ask you, I said . . .

KAY. I was brought up in Niddrie.

LISA. Yes but you wouldn't choose to live there would you I
mean . . . (*Stops herself.*) I'm sorry.

KAY. O.K.

LISA. He's known me since I was eighteen. If he doesn't want
me where could I go?

KAY. Maybe you should . . .

LISA (*interrupts*). He's not impotent you know.

KAY. What?

LISA. He's not impotent. It's not that he can't, he won't. He
just won't. Sometimes I feel him, at night, breathing as if
he's sleeping but lying there hard and burning, then he turns
away from me, rolls over and pulls his knees up like a baby,
like he's protecting himself. It feels like he's punishing me.

KAY. What for?

LISA. For not making him feel beautiful and special and loved.

KAY. Don't you?

LISA. Oh no, I scream at him, pour rage over him like chip fat
and then throw matches.

KAY. Why?

LISA. To punish him.

KAY. What for?

LISA. Not making me feel beautiful and special and loved.

KAY. You are beautiful.

LISA. It ought to be easy. I want to be easy. I do. Just to touch
. . . That's all, just to touch . . . so easy . . . mouths and hands
and skin . . . connected. Slide in and out of each other like
there was no distance between us at all. With your eyes shut

there's no distance to reach across at all . . . I can join in . . .
(*Looks at* KAY.) How drunk am I?

KAY *shakes her head.*

I'm really drunk. I'm really drunk now.

KAY (*gentle*). Better stop then eh?

LISA. Can I stay?

KAY. 'Course you can, as long as you like.

LISA. Can I stay with you? Can I be with you?

KAY *stops stroking her, suddenly wary.* LISA *looks up at her.*

LISA. Don't you want me?

KAY. It's not that . . .

LISA. It's always that. Don't you want me?

KAY. It's complicated.

LISA. I don't *want* it to be complicated!

LISA *hugs* KAY *fiercely.* KAY *strokes her back again.*

KAY. Alright . . . alright come on then, we'll just have a wee
lie down . . . just a cuddle.

KAY *leads her into the inner room.*

Lighting change.

The doors open and light spills out. LISA *comes out of the
room and walks onto the stair. She stands for a moment.*
BOBBY *appears at the bottom of the stairs,* KAY *at the top.*
*They are both looking at her. She looks from one to the
other. They speak softly, gently, smiling at her.*

BOBBY. What have you got under your coat Lisa?

KAY. What have you got on under your coat?

BOBBY. Come on . . .

KAY. Tell us . . .

BOBBY. You can tell us.

LISA. Nothing.

BOBBY. I know.

KAY. You've nothing on.

BOBBY. Nothing but your skin.

KAY. And it's beautiful Lisa.

BOBBY. It's beautiful.

LISA *covers her ears.*

KAY. It's alright.

BOBBY. It's O.K. darlin'.

KAY. You can show us.

LISA (*muttering*). Oh she's not fooling anyone, she is not, walking round like she's wrapped up in cling film, like she pees disinfectant and sweats bleach, she's *desperate*.

BOBBY. Come on.

KAY. Show us Lisa.

LISA. She's got a starved little cat in her, sitting up and begging on the dustbins, clawing for it, yowling for it *begging* for it.

BOBBY. It's beautiful.

KAY. Beautiful Lisa.

LISA. She's desperate, she's filthy she's *pathetic!*

BOBBY. We can see you.

KAY. We can touch you.

LISA (*screaming*). Leave me alone! Leave me alone!

She runs into the flat and bangs the door.

Lighting change. LISA *looks round, dazed for a minute then starts manically tidying up the room, she begins by picking stuff up and finishes by dusting things with a hanky, polishing with her sleeve.* KAY *appears at the inner door, watches her for a second.*

KAY. What are you doing?

LISA (*jumps*). I was just tidying up a bit.

KAY (*a statement rather than a question*). Before you leave.

LISA. I'll need to get back, Brian'll wonder where I've got to.

KAY. Oh.

LISA. I didn't think you were awake.

KAY. I wasn't.

LISA *dusts off her hands, looks round.*

LISA (*brisk*). Well, that'll save you some work in the morning. So I'll see you . . .

KAY. You don't have to go.

LISA. Oh I've an early start tomorrow, stock taking, I'll have everything to do.

KAY. You're shaking, pet. Sit down till you stop shaking, I'll make you a cup of cocoa. (*Reaches out to her.*)

LISA (*evading the touch*). You shouldn't have made me do that, you shouldn't have asked me to do that.

KAY. I didn't ask you to do anything.

LISA. You know what I mean.

KAY (*quiet*). I didn't ask you to do anything. You asked me.

LISA. No.

KAY. Yes you did.

LISA. And what have you got that mirror for?

KAY. What?

LISA. That mirror! That mirror watching everything. What's that about? Watching everything!

KAY. You mean my *dressing* table?

LISA. What have you got that there for? I saw you, looking at me. Looking up and seeing us . . . like that. *Smiling.*

KAY. You were smiling. You were.

LISA. No! God I was drunk. I'm sorry but you can't turn five glasses of brandy and all that . . . nonsense into some kind of love affair, some kind of grand . . . *passion*. You think I wanted to do that? You think I . . .

KAY. I know you did.

LISA. You don't know anything! You don't know anything about me. Don't tell me you know what I want because you haven't a *clue*. Don't you tell me what I feel. I needed a bit of comfort, a bit of friendship and you want to tell me I'm a . . . You stick to your girlfriend. Leave me alone!

KAY. She dumped me. She dumped me in the pub last night. She said she didn't want anything committed. I think that means my daughter. See, no-one likes playing houses and families 'cept those of us who've no got a choice.

LISA. Well I'm sorry that's not my problem. You've got your friends.

KAY. I've nothing. No-one to touch, no-one to watch me sleep, no-one to use for warmth, nothing, just Tina and my garden . . . but I'll tell you, I've more than you.

You lie, don't you? You lie, about everything. It's yourself you're lying to. You're in a bad way, pet.

LISA *stares at her for a moment.*

LISA. Well . . . easy to see why you ended up in the Royal isn't it?

KAY *flinches.*

And by the way you should clean out your fridge. The salad basket is a disgrace.

LISA *exits, appears on the stair. She runs halfway down then stops, her face working, close to tears. KAY is also immobile till the baby cries off, she exits into the inner room. LISA slowly sits down and puts her head on her knees.*

There is movement at the foot of the stairs. BOBBY appears, crawling laboriously upwards, his breathing is laboured, he leaves a trail of blood. As he moves painfully up the stairs MRS MACKIE appears at the top of them staring down at him. She is carrying a coal shovel.

MRS MACKIE. He's suffering. Poor boy. He's suffering.

LISA *runs quickly down to* BOBBY. *She touches him.* BOBBY *groans.* KAY *appears behind* MRS MACKIE, *staring down.*

KAY. Jesus God!

LISA. Get an ambulance! (*As* KAY *hesitates.*) Get an ambulance!

KAY runs back upstairs.

MRS MACKIE. And look at the state of the stair now, I told you to fix it. I've been looking in on him all day, he's no deid yet. I thought you were going to fix it.

LISA. What?

MRS MACKIE. He crawled all the way down those steps, bloody handprints on every step, then he goes and hides in the cupboard under the stairs with the lawnmower. Raving away about rabbits and money lenders and bleeding all over the tarpaulin. Well I'd no strength left had I? There's only so much you can do.

Pause.

LISA. He was here, last night.

MRS MACKIE. Aye!

LISA. What did you do, Mrs Mackie?

MRS MACKIE. I hit him! With my bucket! Aye you don't clean these stairs for forty years without you get some strength in your arms.

MRS MACKIE pushes past LISA impatiently.

Och here I'll need to finish this off myself. (*She raises her shovel over BOBBY.*)

LISA. NO!

MRS MACKIE. Well you do it then! It needs done. (*Hands shovel to LISA.*)

LISA. Why? Why did you hit him?

MRS MACKIE. He was going to dig up the garden, you said so!

LISA. But . . .

MRS MACKIE. He was going to dig up John!

LISA. John's in Canada, Mrs Mackie.

MRS MACKIE. He is not. That was that cheeky bessom in the ground flat started that story, just because I couldn't do things right, have a funeral and a nice stone for him. Just because *she* couldny keep a man longer than a holiday weekend. Well my John never left me, he's dead. He died and I put him under the rose bushes. Then that dog's taking bones out of there . . . *bones!* I *told* you all this this morning lassie, were you no listening?

BOBBY *groans. Pause. Both woman stare down at him as if seeing him properly for the first time.*

Oh God will you not end it? He's suffering, listen to him, he's suffering. John never suffered, it was his heart, he never even opened his eyes except just the once. I brought him his tea at six in the morning just as I always did and he opened his eyes and looked at me, so I told him, 'I can't get the doctor in John because I can't get out of the house, I've my floors to wash today.' I don't know if he heard me, I did my floors and then I sat with him till it was over. Well I couldny get the doctor in then, could I? He'd've known it wasny quick, he'd've asked why I hadny given John his pills. So, when it was good and dark I took him down and put him under the roses, he was a wee man, wasny much worse than bringing a sack of coal in . . . He loved his roses. This boy should've let him be, then he wouldny be suffering now. Oh lassie will you not fix it for me?

It was the way he was! You couldny say no to him, you just couldny, and I was his wife, that's the way it is, I was his *wife*, but it was every night, I'd beg him for peace but it just made him angry, because it was his right, he wanted his rights, every night, I couldny say no to him and he's wanting to go to Canada! Canada! I'd've had no one, not even my things, a strange house and strange people and no even my sister to bring me my messages when I couldn't get out because the sky was too big, there'd've been no-one but him and his routine, his Garibaldi biscuits and his bed . . . I couldny even get down to the end of the street with my nerves! I canny stand it lassie! I canny stand it!

LISA. No.

MRS MACKIE. It's the quiet one's are the worst . . . He got so angry! I couldny refuse him, but he was angry anyway, says

if I wouldny enjoy it there was plenty women that would
and I used to pray he'd go to one of them, one of the hoors
at the docks and give me *peace!*

Looks at BOBBY *again.*

But I never meant harm to him. He shouldny suffer. He's
suffering, lassie.

LISA *bends over the body.*

LISA. He's stopped breathing. He's stopped breathing.

MRS MACKIE. That's it over then. That's it finished with. I'll
away and get a bucket so we can clean up.

MRS MACKIE *goes up the stairs.* LISA *looks down at*
BOBBY, *she bends to touch him, stroking him. Behind her*
BRIAN *and* KAY *have entered from the stair and stair*
door respectively. They stand watching.

LISA. Look what I've done Brian, look what we've done now.

BRIAN *stares. As* LISA *moves away from* BOBBY's *body*
KAY *bends over it and starts to cry.*

Blackout.

Lights up.

MRS MACKIE *is on the stairs in her coat.* LISA *is close to*
her ready to guide her downstairs.

MRS MACKIE. I haveny even been to the corner shop in the
last ten years.

LISA. I know.

MRS MACKIE. The sky's so big. Can you imagine how big
the sky would've been in Canada? Can you imagine the size
of a sky there'd've been over a prairie? Nothing but dust and
sky . . . He wouldny see that though, he wouldny listen.

What'll they do to me?

LISA. I don't know.

MRS MACKIE. They'll lock me up won't they?

LISA. I don't think . . . I don't think you'll need to go to prison.
I'll tell them. I'll tell them what happened, Mrs Mackie. It
was me too. I lied. I lied, Mrs Mackie.

MRS MACKIE. They're waiting down there?

LISA. I'll come with you.

MRS MACKIE. But there's still all this on the stair, someone'll need to clean it, tell them that needs done, look at the mess on it now.

LISA. Alright I'll do it. You go down. I'll clean the stair.

LISA *moves to start mopping.*

I'll take care of it Mrs Mackie. Do you want to wait for me?

MRS MACKIE. Oh I canny keep them waiting. Do you want any messages while I'm out?

LISA. No. We're alright thanks.

MRS MACKIE *moves to exit, looks back at* LISA *cleaning the stair.*

MRS MACKIE. It's no your turn.

LISA. So who's counting?

FUGUE

To Edward

Characters

KAY ONE: A secretary. About 24, frightened and depressed.

KAY TWO: KAY ONE'S memory.

GHOST. Something that wears the shape of a woman about 24-25.

PSYCHIATRIST. Played by the same actress as the GHOST. About 24-25. Self-confident and successful.

Setting

Act One takes place in an isolated cottage near the Ladder Hills, Grampian. There is a bed, bedside lamp, mirror. A few of Kay's belongings are strewn about, half unpacked. Act Two takes place in a hospital ward a few days later. Hospital bed, medical charts, etc.

Fugue was first performed at the Traverse Theatre, Edinburgh, on Thursday, 28 April, 1983, with the following cast:

KAY ONE	Gaylie Runciman
KAY TWO	Kath Rogers
GHOST and PSYCHIATRIST	Evelyn Langland

Directed by Les Waters

Designed by Helen Turner

Lighting design by George Tarbuck

ACT ONE

Scene One

Dark. A GIRL's VOICE *is singing, far away:*
Queen Mary, Queen Mary my age is sixteen
My faither's a fermer on yonder green.
He's plenty o' money tae dress me sae braw
But there's nae bonny laddie will tak me awa.

KAY 2 *is standing in a spotlight.*

*There is the sound of an electric typewriter, faint at first
then growing to almost deafening volume; as it dies away
other sounds surge in waves.*

MAN'S VOICE. Kay? Take some dictation will you? Dear
sir with reference to your letter of the sixteenth . . . sixteenth . . . sixteenth . . .

GIRL. Kay's away on her holidays, (*Giggle.*) Kay's away on
her holidays, (*Giggle.*) Kay's away . . .

*A radio playing music drowns the voices and is in turn
replaced by the sound of a train growing louder and louder.
Suddenly it stops.*

KAY 2 *gasps and shudders as though emerging from deep
water. There is a brief silence. Then in the darkness there is
the distinct sound of someone running their finger along the
edge of a pack of cards.* KAY 2 *peers in the direction of the
noise.*

Light grows to reveal GHOST *sprawled in a chair. She is
staring at* KAY 2.

KAY 2 *walks up to her. The* GHOST *stops and turns away
from her to stare front. She shuffles the cards. The light
fades.*

KAY 1 *walks into the spotlight. She is wearing a grimy
battered dressing gown. Her feet are bare and bandaged.
She looks haggard and starved.*

KAY 1. Everyone wants explanations. (*Shrugs.*) Well I'm not mad, that's the first thing, I'm not mad. I don't see why people can't think of it as a natural phenomenon, what happened, like a tidal wave or an earthquake . . .if they'd found me in this state after an earthquake no-one would be pestering me to know why would they? . . . I think it's easier to think of me as unstable . . . more comfortable all round . . . maybe I am at that. (*Lights up cigarette.*)

Look, it all happened in my head. How am I supposed to explain that? How am I supposed to start describing that? It was real. It wasn't a delusion, a figment of my hysterical imagination. It was *real* . . . but . . . only in *here*. (*Taps her head.*) Do you see? Great. (*To herself.*) That sounds stable doesn't it? (*Bitterly.*)

All that stuff about hauntings, that was the papers. I suppose I was talking a bit wildly at first, they must have got it from that. That place isn't haunted. It's beautiful. It's quite . . . innocent.

I went there to be alone, I admit that. Everyone seems to think there's something unhealthy about wanting a bit of solitude. I was fed up, no, not manically depressed, nothing like that just . . . I've got a really boring job you know . . . I just wanted a change. Sometimes I like being by myself, to think things out. Everyone does that. And this place . . . it's special. It's like . . . part of my childhood I suppose. We went there every summer till I was sixteen. I hadn't been back since.

I'd go there again you know. I would. Even after what . . . (*Stops herself.*) It's a beautiful place. It was my special place.

An alarm clock goes off. Sudden sunlight reveals KAY 2 *in bed, buried in the sheets beyond the reach of the noise. Her hand comes out and hits the clock. After a few moments she sticks her head out and squints at it.*

KAY 2 (*wonderingly*). Half past nine.

KAY 1. They were all knee deep in dictation already. I could lie there till ten o'clock if I wanted to. Midday even.

KAY 2. Don't want to. (*Shambles out of bed.*)

KAY 1. All that free time. I could lie there and doze it all away if I chose.

KAY 2. No I don't. (*Shuffles for bathroom.*) Long lies huh?

KAY 1. Two starlings on the sill, wings glazed with light. The stones sparkled with a late frost.

KAY 2 (*running water*). Cher-ist! (*Wails.*) It's cold !

KAY 1. Outside, wet bald hills and fields, old grass, yellow green. Watery ground and watery light . . . familiar ground . . .

KAY 2 (*singing off*). All things bright and beautiful all creatures great and . . . Towel! What have you done with the *towel* Kay Douglas? (*Staggers back in with eyes screwed shut, wipes face on bedclothes.*) Must unpack sometime. (*Starts making bed.*)

KAY 1. I felt great. First day of the holidays. Like school holidays again. I felt free. I hadn't even unpacked yet. I could suit myself.

KAY 2 (*imitating employer*). 'I do think you should apply yourself more Miss Douglas.' (*Sticks out tongue.*) Bleh.

KAY 1. My job you see . . . well they like to keep you busy. If there's no real work to do they make you dust shelves or something. Clean shelves. That sort of thing annoys me.

KAY 2. 'It's time you realised nine tenths of all work constitutes a form of drudgery Miss Douglas.' Bleh and more bleh.

KAY 1. I mean it's my life, but I've sold them eight hours a day. They have to use them somehow . . . They didn't even want me to take a holiday. 'March is our busiest month Miss Douglas, we can ill spare your services, erratic though they may be.'

KAY 2. You owe me you old mole. Five working days bought and paid for and carried over from last year . . . (*Singing extravagantly.*) All things bright and beootiful . . . Oooooh . . . (*Lies back on bed.*) I'm not going to unpack. Ever.

KAY 1. That was the first thing they latched on to. Why did you go off on your own? Were you upset about something? (*Walks over to look down at* KAY 1.) I wasn't upset. I was glad to be there. I mean I'd been upset. Things had been really getting to me. Well . . . my job mainly . . .

KAY 2. Never going back. Never, never, NEVER! (*Laughs.*) Well, not for seven days.

KAY 1. It 's always the same.

They speak rapidly, independently. Occasionally their lines overlap.

KAY 2 (*chanting*). Read letters, type letters . . .

KAY 1. Make coffee.

KAY 2. File letters, tear up letters . . .

KAY 1. Make coffee.

KAY 2. Redirect letters, decipher illegible letters . . . take a phone call and another and another . . .

KAY 1 . . . . and make coffee and make coffee and more coffee . . .

KAY 2. Well no more!

KAY 1. Not for a week. (*Pause.*) It's always the *same*. Another eight hours. Another pebble on the beach . . . unchanging . . . undramatic . . .

KAY 2 (*bouncing to her feet again looking through possessions, sings*). When you're smiling, when you're smiling . . . Shoes, that's what I need. (*Searches for shoes.*)

KAY 1. The franking machine was the worst. I hated it. I was buried in a basement all alone with it like some kind of obscene arranged marriage – me, fresh young and nubile tied forever to this overweight, farting geriatric who ate paper.

KAY 2 (*singing, putting on shoes*). When you're laughing, when you're laughing . . .

KAY 1. It wasn't the job. It was me. I loathed it . . . but in a quiet sort of way. A numb lazy sort of way . . . that's what gnawed at me. I still trotted in there and sat in that chair and typed and stared out the window . . .

KAY 2 (*raucous*). When you're smiling, when you're smi-el-ing, the whole world smiles with . . . COMB!

Where's my bloody comb! (*Peers under things.*) Cooee, comby, where are you?

KAY 1. Sometimes I think my life has just been a succession of windows. School, college, other jobs . . . Grubby windows with broken Venetian blinds and the drone of French verbs being conjugated over and over. The fan glass of what was once a Georgian mansion, looking out at a green statue of Prince Albert now covered in bird shit, my fingers type dancing the time away . . . my last job, a tiny skylight . . . clouds and cats and pigeons staring down at this pale preserved exhibit who stared back with the strip light making her face a blank . . . Working under that strip light all day gives you a headache.

KAY 2 (*now tugging at her hair in front of mirror*). I feel pretty, oh so pretty, I feel pretty and witty and . . . yeuch! (*Examines plook.*)

KAY 1. I don't see why what I thought about my work was important. O.K. I was a bit bored. Who isn't? Why does everyone keep going on about it?

The light comes up slightly on the GHOST. *She is humming 'Queen Mary' softly.*

KAY 2. (*finishing at mirror*). Don't worry Kay dear, no-one's going to see you, not a soul. (*Freezes.*)

KAY 1. It's not important all that. People keep trying to get me talking about it . . . I suppose it seems tidy, I was bored so I had a nervous breakdown: 'I just thought it would help pass the time doctor' . . . Christ . . . Look, (*Walks up to* KAY 2.) I felt fantastic.

KAY 2 (*still staring blankly forward*). Not a soul.

KAY 1 *turns to look at* GHOST. GHOST *stops humming.*

KAY 1 (*insistently*). I *wanted* a bit of peace and quiet. I did. I've always *liked* my own company . . . (GHOST *disappears again.*)

It's not that I don't have friends or anything.

I could have gone skiing that month. My mate Sheila had asked me . . .

All my close friends, old friends had sort of . . . gone . . .

like I'd sat still and watched them all dash past and vanish
over the horizon . . . running for other jobs, other towns,
other friends . . . going abroad . . .

KAY 2. Saudi Arabia.

KAY 1. I felt like I'd been left out . . . Left behind . . .

Sometimes I get this strange feeling, just the first seconds
before I get out of bed . . . Like a hunger, but every bit of
me, every cell of me's hungry—my mouth to be filled, my
eyes to cry or laugh, all my skin itches to be touched, to
move, to stretch . . . and nothing will ever be *enough*.

KAY 2 (*interrupting suddenly and decisively*). Breakfast. (*She
starts eating.*)

KAY 1. I suppose what I'm really trying to say is I don't think
I had any kind of breakdown. I'd no reason. I'm not like
that. Well look at me! (*Points to* KAY 2.) Do I look
manically depressed?

Oh I don't know.

There's been a lot of speculation about what I 'saw' . . .
I don't see why I have to talk about it, still . . . It seems an
idea that appeals to everyone, poor defenceless young girl
in lonely cottage preyed on by something 'wild and woolly
from the woods' and I quote believe it or not.

I *love* those woods.

KAY 2 *is pulling on a coat still chewing.*

I mean, I did see . . . something. It . . . it was that first day . . .
I went out.

KAY 2. Out.

KAY 1. Drenched four warm limbs in cold air. A small wood.
It was my forest . . . dead leaves, black, damp, halfway to
earth, smell like spice . . .

KAY 2. This is where I was an outlaw . . . this is where I was an
Indian with a twisted bow . . . this is where I was a tiger . . .

KAY 1. A pine branch, a spray of sharp water in my face. The
old paths are still here. Eight years. It's a different
generation of rabbits keeping them clear. I'm too broad to
get down them untangled, I don't quite fit . . .

KAY 2 (*noticing it*). The cave.

KAY 1. Not a real cave, a hollow under ancient roots of broom, big enough to crouch in . . . stuff myself with hoarded food, write curses in fake blood for posterity . . .

KAY 2 (*bending to touch them*). Rusted cans . . .

KAY 1 . . . .and make plans . . .

KAY 2. I'm going to be a nurse, a rock star, a rally driver . . .

KAY 1. Even that last year, hours of staring at the leaves, dreaming my future away . . .

KAY 2. Take my exams and travel the world . . .

KAY 1. Oh yes, that wood was haunted, by me, at nine and six and twelve and sixteen . . . We'd come here every year, I knew every inch.

KAY 2. Funny being back.

KAY 1. I don't quite . . . fit.

Light comes up slowly on GHOST *again.*

And it had its share of the wild and woolly. A schoolfriend used to feed me horror stories. All my nightmares were peopled with cheap sensational images: Victorian bread and butter writers reaching out of paupers' graves to stroke my spine with shabby tales of demons and strangulation.

KAY 2 (*pulling a face*). Woooo! (*Giggles.*)

KAY 1. There's one path in the wood, a tunnel through overhanging branches . . .

KAY 2. Don't look back.

KAY 1. If you looked back . . . it got you.

KAY 2 (*giggling again*). It.

KAY 1. Don't ask me what 'it' was . . . just . . .

KAY 2. Something horrible. (*Fake fiendish cackle.*)

KAY 1. No. If I'd looked back and seen an empty path . . . nothing at all . . . that would have been the worst . . . Nothing there at all.

The GHOST *snaps a twig in her hands.* KAY 2 *spins to stare at her.*

KAY 2. Hell's teeth . (*Catches her breath.*) Don't be silly.
Don't be silly. There's nothing there.

KAY 1. Eight years and I still jumped. They call it an over
active imagination. Well it was all the same . . . I ran and
jumped and rolled in it all. My wood. Got it down my neck
and in my shoes and under my finger nails . . .

KAY 2 (*pulls a face*). Damp.

KAY 1. It was good. I climbed my mountain. A small grassy
hill. I'd lie alone on top of it and stare down and think of
nothing at all, just look . . .

KAY 2. Right foot, left foot, (*Pants.*) come on Kay, without a
break, climb it in one, right foot, left foot . . . Now . . .
(*Looks round her breathing quickly.*)

KAY 1. A long stretch of ground. Bog and moor. A blanket of
greens and browns and bright streamers of water. My little
kingdom. Not another living soul for miles . . .

KAY 2. Who's *that?*

KAY 1. They were walking, a small dark figure far below me
on the wide flat ground. Walking, but never getting any
closer . . . only the legs treading the ground, as if the earth
was moving under their feet and they were treading against
it . . .

KAY 2. Who?

KAY 1. An anonymous doll-like figure pacing . . . nowhere.

Light fades on GHOST.

Then it . . . (*Hastily.*) it must have got beyond a rise in the
ground. They must have walked out of sight . . . It vanished.
I thought . . .

KAY 2. Maybe they were walking into the wind . . .

KAY 1. There was a light breeze high on the hill where I
stood. It lifted grey stuff, all some fox or hawk had left of
a rabbit, and batted it gently to and fro among the grass
stems . . .

KAY 2 *stands staring at where the* GHOST *was.*

That's it, that's all. Finish.

I'm telling you, that's all I saw, all of it. The rest was just dreams. Just in my head.

(*Smiles.*) Nobody wants to hear that. They all want something more. O.K. . . . I have seen other things . . . At the age of five . . .

KAY 2. A little old lady.

KAY 1 . . . . standing in the cloakroom of my kindergarten school. Just standing there beneath the pegs and rows of little green coats . . .

KAY 2 . . . . the smell of used gym shoes . . .

KAY 1. You don't smell dreams. They hung her portrait on the wall months later . . . Founder's portrait . . .

KAY 2. Dead one hundred years exactly.

KAY 1. So maybe I had seen it somewhere else.

KAY 2. This is different. This feels . . .

KAY 1. 'Ms. Douglas, is it or is it not a fact that on the thirtieth of July 1976, you being at the time some seventeen years of age, you saw a further apparition while employed as a castle guide in a genuine medieval castle? To what do you attribute this apparition?'

KAY 2 (*reflectively*). Sex.

KAY 1. 'Sex?'

KAY 2. Makes sense. I mean it was all starting to happen at that age wasn't it? I was quite . . . keyed up about everything . . .

KAY 1. 'You attributed this image of a person dead some two hundred years to the vibrations of an overactive libido?'

KAY 2. Well . . . (*Weighs the idea up.*) . . . His portrait was quite attractive . . . I suppose I could have made the whole thing up . . .

KAY 1. 'Created the vision yourself in a frenzy of sexual fervour? Were you in a frenzy of sexual fervour?'

KAY 2. I was doing the cleaning. Hmmm. (*Shakes her head.*)

KAY 1. There's been other things like that. Little things. So that figure walking . . . I'd seen other things like that. I never told anyone. Oh it's just nerves. I'm highly strung. Fatigue. Over caffeination . . . What used to worry me is that it might show. That it was written in neon across my forehead: 'I think I have had psychic experiences. Classified Loonie.' Tell anyone and they start watching you sideways waiting for you to hang from the Venetian blind saying you're a pickled onion. The thing is . . . what happened . . . the dreams whatever . . . it wasn't like that . . .

KAY 2. I felt it. (*She takes coat off and goes to sit in chair. Light fades.*)

KAY 1. Do I have to talk about this? I don't think it will make me feel better. I think I'll remember. I don't want to remember . . . All right! All right. (*Rapidly.*) That day, I was caught in the rain. No shelter. Every twig and leaf was sodden, I got damper layer by layer. Glorious discomfort. A hot bath, a warm fire and I dozed in front of it. Sleeping where I sat.

(*Agitated.*) That's reason enough for waking at two a.m., the fire dead, every muscle cramped. That's how you get nightmares isn't it? The body's trying to scare you into waking up and making it comfortable.

Yeah?

Everyone has nightmares.

But this was . . . Oh Jesus . . .

KAY 2 (*stirring*). Jesus . . .

KAY 1. It was cold.

KAY 2 (*shudders and sucks in her breath*). . . . Cold.

KAY 1. Dark and black and cold and something . . . something.

The GHOST *walks slowly out of the shadows to stand behind* KAY 2. *She ruffles cards in* KAY 2's *ear.*

KAY 2 *turns and finds her face level with the* GHOST's. *The* GHOST *smiles a slow joyless smile that stays on her face for a few seconds then vanishes abruptly.*

GHOST (*dead*). Kay. (*She looks round her slowly with exaggerated head movements like an animal sizing up a new environment. She makes the name a sound rather than a word.*) Kay. Kay. (*Her eye settles on* KAY 2 *again and she freezes looking at her sideways. Slowly she turns her head till it is level with* KAY 2*'s, nose to nose. Her tongue touches her lip once.*)

Hungry.

After a second she smiles the same joyless smile, she touches KAY 2*'s hair lightly.*

KAY 1. I felt it. I *felt* it.

GHOST (*coaxingly*). Hungry. (*Turns and walks slowly away from* KAY 2 *into the darkness.*)

KAY 2 *remains unmoving. Alarm and daylight arrive suddenly and simultaneously. She sits still for a moment then stiffly gets up to stop alarm as it peters into silence.*

KAY 2. I suppose . . . ?

KAY 1. I suppose I slept.

KAY 2. I *must* have slept . (*Sits down on bed.*)

KAY 1. It was a grey day. Low cloud a lid on the horizon, hanging, waiting to drop and suffocate the ground in mist. A damp, dull grey day. And I didn't bother to put fresh clothes on. So. That was the dream. One of the dreams. Not very healthy I suppose. So I had tangible ones. (*Shrugs.*)

I was upset, depressed, whatever. A bit. It didn't work, coming back. I thought I'd like it, nostalgia for all the good times I had. It didn't help . . . remembering didn't help . . .

KAY 2 (*quiet*). I'm going to be a rock star, a rally driver . . .

KAY 1. Type letters, file letters, make coffee . . .

KAY 2. Take my exams and travel the world . . .

KAY 1. The seconds of my life ticking away They're precious those moments, precious as blood . . .

KAY 2. Something wild, something *special* . . .

KAY 1. I'm not very special.

Maybe my nightmares are unique. Well . . . I better cultivate them then.

Don't you think? (*Shakes her head.*)

No. I tried to work it out sitting there. I was *scared*.

KAY 2. I felt it.

KAY 1. It's not my job, it's me. It's all of it. It's my life. Idling down the plughole, second by second . . .

KAY 2. I could get run over by a bus tomorrow. (*Smiles.*)

KAY 1. What would it change? I had a row . . . discussion with Sheila about it.

KAY 2 (*bitterly*). Sheila.

KAY 1 (*imitation of Sheila*). 'Your trouble is you worry too much.'

KAY 2. No but listen, I mean it! If I did who'd notice? What difference would it make? There I'd be wandering along, thinking I about what I was going to have for tea, or what I wanted to do at the weekend, or how I was going to be world famous one day, and then 'splat!' I'd be a smear on the tarmac and a few fantasies vanishing into the ether. Don't you see?

KAY 1. She didn't.

KAY 2. It makes everything pointless. Everything. We're wasting time.

KAY 1. Do I believe that? (*Frowns, considering it.*) Sometimes I enjoy playing lonely and misunderstood you know?

KAY 2. This is different. This is real. (*Light fades on KAY 2 in bed.*)

KAY 1. Oh no. Don't drag all this up. Don't. I don't want to think about it. Don't! (*The GHOST walks over to the bed. She hums 'Queen Mary'.*)

KAY 2 (*wakes up*). Jesus . . . ? (*Stares at GHOST.*)

GHOST (*gentle*). Kay.

KAY 2. What are you? What's going on?

GHOST. Kay.

KAY 2. I'm dreaming. It's a dream.

GHOST. Hungry. *I'm* hungry. (*Smiles, moves slowly to sit on bed.*)

KAY 2. I'm dreaming that's all. All right Kay. All right . . . .
just switch on the light, that's it, reach out and switch it
on . . . (*Eyes on* GHOST *she reaches blindly for light
switch.*) Come on.

The GHOST *puts her hand over the light switch.* KAY 2
*stares down at it for a second then reaches out and touches
it. The* GHOST *grabs her hand.* KAY 2 *makes a small
terrified noise. Blackout.*

KAY 1. Don't.

Lights up on scene as before. GHOST *humming.*

KAY 1. No!

KAY 2. What?

GHOST. Hungry.

KAY 2. Who are you?

GHOST. Kay.

KAY 1. No!

GHOST. Kay.

KAY 2 *reaches for the light switch again.* GHOST *stops
her as before, moving more rapidly this time. Blackout.*

KAY 1. Don't.

Lights up. GHOST *sitting on bed.* KAY 2 *reaching for the
light switch.*

KAY 2. No.

KAY 1. No!

KAY 2. Oh please don't.

KAY 1. DON'T!

The GHOST *grabs* KAY 2. KAY 1 *screams.* GHOST *and*
KAY 2 *freeze staring at each other.* GHOST *gets up slowly
and walks over to behind* KAY 1 *who is standing face
buried in her hands.* GHOST *pauses for a second then
moves off slowly.* KAY 1 *raises her head .* KAY 2 *is still
frozen.*

KAY 1 (*whispers*). Every night. (*Walks to look at* KAY 2.)
Every night. WHY?

KAY 2. What's wrong with me?

KAY 1. Something out of the dark. Tracking me. Scenting me. Hunting me. Coming right through my head. Something was smashing holes in there and struggling up into my dreams. Getting closer. The dreams were first like a warning breath on my neck.

Daylight grows on KAY 2 *again.*

You should have got up then, You should have just got up with the daylight and run off. Get out!

KAY 2. What's wrong with me?

KAY 1. Oh Kay.

Pause.

KAY 2: (*sits up*). I'm just a bit overtired that's all.

KAY 1 (*bitterly*). Oh yes. That's right.

KAY 2. I've been letting things get on top of me.

KAY 1. Shovelling them on to your head with an earth mover.

KAY 2. It doesn't matter. I'll go home. Tomorrow. I'll go home. (*Sobs.*) What for? What'll I do there?

KAY 1. Anything, you can do *anything*.

KAY 2. I won't be back, what difference does it make?

KAY 1. Jesus! You! YOU! A nervous breakdown? (*To audience.*) You think she had a nervous breakdown? *Her?* She'd have loved it. Revelled in it. Conclusive proof that she was something special. Highly strung. Unusually unstable. Different. But she's not . (*Yells at* KAY 2.) You're not! What were you doing shutting yourself away in that cottage, brooding your time away? What were you trying to prove? Look what you did to me because you were *bored*. Just because life wasn't spoiling you the way I thought it would. Didn't you realise what was happening?

I see things. And I knew I did. I knew what was happening to me, inside, deep down, I knew. I stayed out of pride. Stupid pride. I was proud I could terrify myself with visions. I wanted to hover on the brink of sanity.

Because it was something wild, something special.

Because it was happening to *me*.

You stupid cow Kay Douglas!

White noise starts in the background, quiet at first then growing louder.

KAY 1. Oh no.

(*The noise grows, over* KAY 2*'s voice heard speaking childishly.*) I'm going to be a rock star, a rally driver, an Indian, a tiger . . .

KAY 1. I don't want to think about it!

(KAY 2*'s voice is now repeating.*) What difference does it make? What difference does it make?

KAY 2 *gets to her feet.* KAY 1 *moves away from the bed, panting, her hands on her face.* KAY 2 *follows, moving identically.*

The noise is now the GHOST *repeating* 'Hungry, hungry, hungry . . . '

The GHOST *walks into* KAY 2*'s path. Both* KAY*'s look up.* KAY 2 *stares horrified at* GHOST, KAY 1 *at empty air. The* GHOST *takes* KAY 2*'s hand.* KAY 1 *raises hers as if it too is being held.* GHOST *suddenly pulls on* KAY 2*'s arm and grabs her. Noise stops.*

KAY 1. Kay no! (*Whirls to look at* GHOST *and* KAY 2.)

GHOST *smiles at her.*

Blackout.

Scene Two

KAY 1 *and* KAY 2 *are standing side by side. The* GHOST *is in the background as before.*

KAY 1. When I was two, I still had a cot. My father dropped me in it, me in my stretch nylon pyjamas with little yellow animals all over them, and talked me to sleep, with stories about rabbits.

KAY 2. When I was two I was given a large cuddly rabbit of my own.

KAY 1. I ate it. Right down to the little plastic rose.

KAY 2. When I was two we went to the cottage for the first time. I saw real rabbits for the first time.

KAY 1. They weren't at all what I expected.

KAY 2. There was a jasmine tree at the back door then. I thought it was magic, flowering when everything was still waking up.

KAY 1. I used to crawl out of bed and sit under it and stare at the moon.

KAY 2. There was a hedgehog used to sit there too. Eating slugs.

KAY 1. My brother found a huge packing case in the shed at the cottage . . .

KAY 2 . . . . when I was five . . .

KAY 1. He sat in it for days. We had to carry his meals out to him.

KAY 2. He said he was going to fly to the moon in it.

KAY 1. I remember feeling slightly surprised when he never took off.

KAY 2. He sat me on his bed and solemnly showed me a great scribble of biro scratches. A wobbly chaos. 'What is it?'

KAY 1. It.

KAY 2. But what is it?

KAY 1. Nothing.

KAY 2. But what is it?

KAY 1. It's *nothing*. That's what nothing looks like. And if it gets you . . .

KAY 2. Yes?

KAY 1. You're nothing.

KAY 2. 'It' lived in attics till I was eight or nine.

KAY 1. It lived in my nightmares longer.

KAY 2. The first tree I ever climbed was the lilac tree at the back of the cottage.

KAY 1. It's a bush.

KAY 2. It was a tree then. Its heart was rotten but strong enough to bear my four-year-old weight.

KAY 1. The next was a broom tree.

KAY 2. That was a bush as well.

KAY 1. A larger one. It grew out of the compost heap. It had a nest full of blackbird's eggs in it when I first climbed it.

KAY 2. They grew old. A smug orange cat sat at the bottom of the tree and licked his whiskers. I hadn't expected the cat.

KAY 1. When I was twelve I climbed the beech tree at the edge of my forest.

KAY 2. It was enormous.

KAY 1. It was quite tall.

KAY 2. It had storeys like a house, a roof of leaves. Climbing to the top was a major expedition. I spent days there . . .

KAY 1 . . . . lying motionless, squinting at the ground.

KAY 2. I was a tiger ready to drop on an antelope, just the tip of my tail twitching.

KAY 1. When I was twelve, I didn't believe I could ever grow out of pretend games . . .

KAY 2. I was a beautiful, savage, Indian squaw waiting to ambush a cowboy who was going to be terribly impressed . . .

KAY 1. Then somehow they grew difficult to believe in . . . I had other dreams.

KAY 2. When I was sixteen I left school. I lay under the beech tree and watched the squirrels chasing their tails, shooting along the branches as though they were on wires.

KAY 1. I felt . . . lucky. It was my life now. There was no reason for it ever to go wrong again.

KAY 2. From the top of my mountain you could see the road in the distance.

KAY 1. A minor road. Grass down its middle.

KAY 2. It wasn't impressive enough to warrant the entrance of a knight on a white charger, but it looked as though it might run to a mildly attractive American tourist.

KAY 1. It was a beautiful summer. The last time I was here. The air was full, light and seeds everywhere. Mist in the morning, dancing midges in the evening.

KAY 2 walks slowly away to sit in chair.

I lay and looked at it all and dreamed about my future. The places I was going to go. The people I would meet. How it was all going to *feel.* I could be anything. *Anything.*

The GHOST *comes to stand at* KAY 2*'s shoulder.* KAY 2 *is staring blankly front.*

KAY 1. How did I get here? To this?

I didn't really believe I was going to be unique, world famous, extraordinary . . .

I always thought I'd *feel* unique.

(*To* KAY 2.) You'd no reason to get into this state! You'd no *right.*

The GHOST *takes out a cigarette from* KAY 2*'s pocket, lights it and puts it in* KAY 2*'s mouth. She lets* KAY 2 *take a puff then removes it again. She feeds her puffs throughout the subsequent action.*

KAY 1. I suppose I just drifted into it . . . I seemed to drift into everything. Sitting, just sitting. Chain smoking. Terrified. What was it Kay? What frightened you? It was just fear, crawling slowly through me like blood moving round my body. Even this place terrified me. My parents met here. That's probably why we kept coming back, reliving memories even then. It was chance, them meeting here—my mother's family and my father had double booked. So they shared. That was another hot summer they tell me. A double booking and a ridge of high pressure and twenty five years later here's Kay Douglas revisiting . . . terrified . . .

Even the light seemed wrong. Just slightly, as though there were a filter on the sun. A trace of sickly colour on everything like a badly developed film. Sometimes it seemed there were too many shadows, or that they were in the wrong places . . . Little things. Nothing definite. Nothing I could be certain of.

And nothing moved.

I sat, like a mouse watching for the twitch of a paw outside the hole, and stared at everything. Nothing moved. Crazy!

I *knew* nothing would.

But neither could I, for terror.

Silence. Ringing in my ears on one note like a distant alarm bell, on and on and on . . . I couldn't move.

(*Walks up to* KAY 2.) Oh I had to move sometimes, let's not exaggerate, I wasn't that far gone. (*Bitterly.*) Didn't eat though did you? I'm still hungry.

It was as if I'd no reason to do anything. As if I'd known the reason once but forgotten what it was.

Oh Kay. Snap out of it! Come on. What's got into you?

KAY 2. What's got into me?

KAY 1. Got inside you, crawled into your head like a snake curling up under a rock. *Stopped* you.

The GHOST *starts humming; she moves forward past* KAY 1 *and gently pushes* KAY 2's *head down to stare at her feet. She strokes the back of* KAY 2's *head gently, all the while watching* KAY 1.

KAY 1. I felt it. It was *real*. A dead weight on my head. I was terrified. There I was, alone, trailing misery like blood in water. Sharks smell a drop of blood thirty miles away. I was leaking fear, staking myself out like raw bait . . . something smelt it.

GHOST *laughs softly.*

(*To* KAY 2.) What were you so scared of?!

KAY 2. Waking up in the dark . . .

KAY 1. *What?*

KAY 2. Waking up in the dark and feeling . . .

KAY 1 (*interrupts*). That was months ago.

KAY 2. Just lying there dozing, fingers idly exploring your own body and there it is.

KAY 1. It was *nothing*.

KAY 2. A lump. No, it was worse than that, two lumps, like little plum stones inside the soft fruit.

KAY 1. They were nothing. They cut them out and they were *nothing*, just benign little blots of fibre. That's all.

KAY 2. They were really there.

KAY 1. What's all the fuss about! That's *stupid*. What were you worrying about *them* for, it was over.

KAY 2. I felt them.

KAY 1. So my skin isn't immune to scalpels and tumours? Whose is? I thought I'd found the seeds of death inside me, who doesn't carry them? I just thought mine were germinating a little early . . .

KAY 2. I never thought it would happen to me.

KAY 1 (*snaps*). Well it can!

It was nothing. A great fuss about nothing.

Look, I wasn't thinking about it really. It was just a bit of a shock at the time, a bit unexpected. You never do think anything like that is going to happen to you.

KAY 2. It could.

KAY 1. Well it didn't!

Pause.

I was brooding about it, depressing myself. I was brooding about it. (*Sighs.*) It's not as simple as that. It's everything.

There was a song I always used to sing, sitting in my beech tree staring at the road. (*Sings.*)

Queen Mary, Queen Mary my age is sixteen,
My faither's a fermer on yonder green,
He's plenty o' money tae dress me sae braw,
But there's nae bonny laddie will take me awa.

That was me, dolled up to the nines and trembling with anticipation, waiting, just waiting for life to hit me. The glorious unexpected. Excitement. I mean when I was sixteen I was thinking mainly in terms of some man dropping out of the sky and chucking flowers at me, but it was everything. Not just that. I was on the brink of it all. I couldn't wait. Now . . .

Here it comes out of the future, the unexpected, thundering down like a juggernaut to squash me flat . (*Looks at* KAY 2.) And here I am like a rabbit, blind and frozen with fear right in the middle of the road . . .

. . . I used to watch people streaming down the street, busy Saturday shopping crowds. Everyone glancing at the faces approaching them, eyes constantly rolling like greased pinballs in their heads, surrounded by the unknown, the unknowable, the potentially unexpected. Like bodyguards packed around American diplomats, eyes constantly on the move looking for killers. Survival instinct I suppose. Except that the unexpected is always that . . . unexpected. The crime writers' cliché, the warm corpse always looks surprised.

I've never seen a corpse, apart from Lenin's. Sheila and me went on a package tour to Moscow . . . Lenin's mummy is the deadest thing I've ever seen, a hunk of very old meat, and the reverence, the endless lines of worshippers (all in black as if they never got over his dying), seem somehow obscene. Thousands of stares falling on it seems to have blurred its edges so that it's melting like wax but the face is very faintly surprised . . . as if this isn't at all what he expected. And he's supposed to have changed history . . .

KAY 2. No-one's in control.

KAY 1. There I was, lying in my safe warm bed, thinking about what colour I was going to paint the living room, where I was going on holiday, and worrying about my overdraft, and there were those lumps inside me. In one split second my mind leaped from exploratory operations to radical mastectomy to death, and that's the future I carried into work and lived with for three weeks. Of course the lumps were there before I invented my morbid little scenario. When they turned out to be benign I abandoned it again. None of my imaginary futures is real. Only the terror is real. (*Looks at* KAY 2.)

KAY 2 (*looks slowly round at* GHOST.) Who are you?

GHOST. Kay.

KAY 1. Stop it !

GHOST. Hungry. (*Opens mouth and breathes out a long slow breath. The sound of white noise starts as if it was the noise the* GHOST *was making. It cuts off at a peak again.*)

KAY 2. A mouth. A great hot mouth, sucking us all down its gullet even while we're still kicking and crying then . . .

KAY 1 (*shouts*). Nothing! . . . Nothing at all.

KAY 2 *stands up. The* GHOST *dresses her in an identical battered dressing gown to* KAY 1*'s.*

KAY 1. No-one's in control. Please . . . I want to stop now . . . I can't tell any more . . . You must understand . . . I can't, I don't know what I felt, how can I tell you? (*Seems to be trying to work it out.*) . . . it was when I was waiting for the test results from the hospital, I took a few days off work and sat at home and scratched my stitches and watched telly. My little trouble was tagging on the skirts of a wave of world disasters. Every time I switched on it showed me twisted limbs and scorched cooked skin, bright foreign rubble and distant dusty explosions . . .

KAY 2 . . . . children on pin-thin legs with huge ancient eyes . . .

KAY 1. And I watched documentaries about world wars and similar slaughters, roomfuls of politicians and historians berating each other with hindsight. It's all so clear in retrospect, pin history on the map with little coloured flags and stab accusing fingers at it and scream 'Why didn't they see?'

KAY 2. Waking up in the dark . . .

KAY 1 (*snort of disgust*). Who am I kidding? I wasn't thinking about world history or worldwide suffering or . . . (*Shakes her head.*) . . . All I cared about was my history, my future . . . my little lumps . . . my little surprise presents . . . I needn't have worried, but I didn't know that . . .

Well there you go folks. Kay Douglas wants to know the answer to it all. Who doesn't? But Kay here wasn't content with just pondering it all in the odd half hour in the bath, oh no, she only had to dream dreams and see visions and scare herself blind and deaf and dumb and *stupid!* . . . (*Turns on* KAY 2.) Didn't you!

The GHOST *pushes* KAY 2 *into the chair again and turns and walks away into the shadows. White noise mixed with the jumbled disjointed sounds of radio, typewriter, train and* KAY 2 *singing start softly and grow to a crescendo during* KAY 1 *'s speech.*

KAY 1. I can't tell you what happened next. I can't . . . I just . . . I don't want to think about it! I *daren't!* (*Hands on face, rocking backwards and forwards speaking quietly, urgently.*) The whole of that room, that safe little room where I knew every scrape on the furniture, the whole of it was hanging over me . . . an unspoken, unknown threat. I *couldn't move.* Watching the day grow, the light getting thinner and greyer . . . the shadows crawling round the floor to lick my feet and suddenly . . . suddenly I thought I was waiting for something, I was sitting *waiting* for one moment, one second when I was going to see . . . I *can't say* it!

KAY 2 (*hands to her ears*). Stop it! Stop it!

KAY 1. Run Kay! RUN!

KAY 2 *runs, falls, stumbles towards* KAY 1 *and hurls herself into her arms. They cling together.* KAY 2 *is shivering and panting.*

KAY 1. I can't tell you what I saw. I don't . . . I just can't. (*To herself.*) It was real. It *was.* (*Closes her eyes for a second, shivers.*) Well . . . that's all of it. After that they found me wandering round and round my mountain as if I was looking for a way in.

KAY 2 (*speaking into* KAY 1*'s shoulder*). Right foot, left foot, right foot, left foot, yes, yes, move, keep moving . . . right foot, left foot.

KAY 1. I was lucky. The woman who owned the cottage just looked in to check on me . . . they found me in just a damp draggled dressing gown with bare bloody feet, wandering, raving, running . . .

KAY 2. Keep moving, keep moving . . .

KAY 1. I was walking in circles. No-one understood that . . .
   I wasn't running away, I was *running*. Just to move, just to
   stumble and gasp and move . . . that *was* escaping.

KAY 2. Right foot, left foot, good, good, good girl. Come on
   now . . .

KAY 1. Before dawn the wind rose, tugging the hair off my
   face, rushing into my lungs. Everything moved, sky and
   ground, struggling with the air, rolling and dancing with
   it . . . and I ran . . .

KAY 2. Move. *Move.*

KAY 1. With the light came gulls. Falling out of the sky,
   yelping and squabbling over fresh damp grubs . . . and I
   yelled and stamped my battered feet.

KAY 2. Come *on* Kay . . .

KAY 1. It was good. It was *good.* Stumbling and sobbing and
   cold and rough and sharp on my legs, water and stone and
   grass . . . I was out of that place, I'd got away . . . Then there
   were hordes of people. Lights everywhere. A clamour of
   voices all at once. Someone made me lie down . . .

KAY 2. Rough warm blankets.

KAY 1. I cried all over them all. Clung to them.

KAY 2. Arms holding me. Hands patting me. 'You're all right
   now.'

KAY 1. Blue lights spinning, ambulance, police, flash bulbs
   exploding . . .

KAY 2. And gulps and gulps and gulps of hot soup . . .

KAY 1. And I slept. When I woke up there were more of them.
   Nurses and journalists and my family . . .

KAY 2. But what happened? What happened? What happened?

KAY 1. I don't *know* . . . ! I don't know. I see things. I scared
   myself, that's all.

KAY 2 *steps out of her arms. They look at each other for a
second then* KAY 2 *exits.*

It's all a big fuss about nothing really. I'm sorry. I blow
things up, get them out of proportion.

Just my own ghosts. My own monsters.

Sheila was in to see me today. I bruised her arms. I couldn't let go: 'Your trouble is you're highly strung.' Maybe.

I saw it though. I *saw* it. Maybe something is there, waiting for us to go and look on it, scenting our fear and coming to suck on it . . . something evil . . . (*Shakes her head abruptly.*)

Look it was nothing really. All in my head. Nothing. I'm sorry . . . I'm . . . I'm sorry.

Pauses for a moment then exits.

ACT TWO

Scene One

PSYCHIATRIST *standing alone in same spot as* KAY 1 *at the start of Act One.*

PSYCHIATRIST. I don't believe in ghosts.

I remember thinking that might be a real handicap, 'cause I had a real fanatic on my hands. I thought it would be like wrestling with a bramble bush trying to get any kind of communication started . . . well . . . this isn't supposed to be an official report . . . you want to know what happened, from my point of view. It's just difficult to know how to start . . . everything's coloured with hindsight now, by what happened.

I suppose it's sheer fluke that I ever ended up by handling Kay Douglas's case at all. I mean I'm not long qualified, I'd only just been appointed to the hospital . . . if anyone had thought she was mentally ill I wouldn't have been handling it unsupervised. The assumption was that she'd had a minor breakdown which precipitated a form of fugue state . . . oh sorry, that's when someone under stress simply starts walking, some people travel 50 miles or more before they're stopped, they just keep moving their legs . . . that's what we thought had happened to Kay. It seemed all she needed was a little rest and reassurance. We wanted to find out what had disturbed her of course . . . and there was the problem of all the publicity surrounding her discovery, but it seemed a very simple case . . .

I was curious, yes, but . . . well all these Sunday paper sensations about the supernatural leave me a bit cold I'm afraid. I can't suspend disbelief long enough to manage even a sympathetic shudder. Something else scared me, something about the way she looked at me . . . I did feel a bit of a twinge when I heard where she'd been found. I used to spend every summer up at Glenbuchat when I was a kid . . . we rented that cottage, it was one of those coincidences that

seem so statistically improbable you end up examining them
from every angle looking for some deeper significance. I
never mentioned that link to Kay Douglas. It worried me.
I suppose she'd created so many of her own associations
for the place . . . frightening ones and . . . I think I felt . . .
jealous in a way. That was my place, my *special* place. Oh
I knew other families stayed there but I managed to forget
that; it was ours, *mine*. Part of my childhood I suppose. I ran
wild up there, made the forest a kind of jungle and roamed
in it playing mad games, came home with twigs in my hair,
blood on my knees and the hunger of a shoal of starved
piranhas.

Always seemed to be summer. Clichéd huh?

I remember the last year we went there, I must have been . . .
sixteen or seventeen . . . I remember the feel of the air when
it was first warm enough to shed the extra layers and *feel* the
air all over. Daytime, the sun licking your flesh like a hot
tongue . . . evening and all that burning skin soothed with
coolness . . . First day of the holidays I used to belt out the
cottage door and run for the big beech tree at the edge of the
wood, legs pumping, shrieking 'Freedom!' at the top of my
lungs before hanging upside down from the branches . . .

So it was a special place, beautiful, beloved and very, very
private. I didn't want to share all that with Kay . . . I suppose
we may have walked and run and lain in the same places
only a day apart, me and Kay . . . It's one of the things that
seems so upsetting now . . . I mean . . . (*Frowns, too upset
suddenly to find words.*)

. . . I don't know how it happened. I don't. I know the
events, the cold facts but there seems something more, so
many coincidences like that . . . only they don't make sense.
I don't know *how* to make sense of them . . .

Lights up slowly on KAY 1 *in bed playing with a pack of
cards.*

And you always think . . . 'Maybe if someone else had
handled that case . . . ?'

And I can't ever know. (*Walks slowly back to* KAY 1 *who is
still absorbed in her game.*)

PSYCHIATRIST (*to* KAY). How are you feeling?

KAY 1. I'm all right. There's nothing wrong with me.

PSYCHIATRIST. Playing patience?

KAY 1. No. So when can I go home?

PSYCHIATRIST. I wouldn't know I'm afraid.

KAY 1. Someone must know.

PSYCHIATRIST. I just wanted to talk to you for a few minutes.

KAY 1 (*looks up sharply*). Press?

PSYCHIATRIST *shakes her head.*

Well who then?

PSYCHIATRIST. Staff.

KAY 1. How do you mean?

PSYCHIATRIST. I just wanted to ask a few questions about your experiences that's all.

KAY 1. Well why? What for? Who are you?

(PSYCHIATRIST *says nothing.*) Look I'm sorry but I've had people in here asking me questions morning noon and night: 'How do you feel? Why weren't you wearing shoes? Does this hurt? Did you see ghosts? Could you roll over while we shove you full of tranquilisers . . . ?' So what do you want?

PSYCHIATRIST. It won't take long.

KAY 1. You're not a psychiatrist are you?

PSYCHIATRIST. I didn't know you'd been seeing one.

KAY 1. I haven't. I don't need to.

PSYCHIATRIST. I'm glad to hear it. Lovely view you have, you're lucky to have a bed by the window.

KAY 1. Yeah. It's hours of endless fun lying here looking at the sky.

PSYCHIATRIST. Why don't you get some papers sent in, listen to the radio or something? (KAY 1 *stares at her coldly then goes on playing with the cards.*

PSYCHIATRIST *consults notes.*) Kay Douglas, age 24, employed as a secretary with firm of Thompson's Entrenching Tools . . .

KAY 1 (*sotto voce*). Thompson's Entrenching Tools. (*Snorts.*)

PSYCHIATRIST. Sorry?

KAY 1. Got a real ring to it hasn't it?

PSYCHIATRIST (*carries on as if she hadn't spoken*). . . . on March 12th you left to spend a week alone at an isolated cottage near Glenbuchat. On March 17th you were found wandering the hillside near the cottage wearing only a dressing gown . . . correct so far?

KAY 1. Look . . . I don't know if I want to go over all this again if you don't mind.

PSYCHIATRIST. You want me to stop?

KAY 1. I don't know . . . It's just . . .

PSYCHIATRIST. I could always come back later.

KAY 1. Oh Christ. No I'll get it over with. (*Lies back and closes her eyes.*)

PSYCHIATRIST (*continues reading from notes*). At the time you made no explanation of your condition apart from several confused statements about an alleged 'haunting' you had experienced at the cottage — medical evidence — shock, exposure . . . minor . . . lacerations . . . to . . . feet . . . (*Writes.*) Now. We think you may have had a very minor breakdown Miss Douglas, it's nothing to worry about. All I want to do is ask you a few questions to see if we can establish what kind of stress you were under. All right? (KAY 1 *remains motionless.*) Well now you'd been somewhat, disillusioned shall we say, with your job hadn't you?

KAY 1 (*sighs 'Oh God here we go again'*). Yes!

PSYCHIATRIST. And you'd recently undergone a minor operation yes?

KAY 1. It was very minor.

PSYCHIATRIST. An exploratory operation for suspected cancer?

KAY 1. They were pretty sure it wasn't you know.

PSYCHIATRIST. Well we've got the details of that on your medical record . . . (*Makes note.*) . . . right . . . Now, you'd recently split up with your boyfriend hadn't you?

KAY 1. *What?*

PSYCHIATRIST. He left to take up a job in Saudi Arabia, is that right?

KAY 1. Who the . . . ! Who told you that? I haven't talked about that!

PSYCHIATRIST. I believe the information came from one of your workmates . . . Sheila . . . Thompson is it?

KAY 1. She didn't. She *wouldn't.*

PSYCHIATRIST (*looks at her for a moment*). Is it true?

KAY 1 (*quiet*). Yes. (*Reaches for her cigarettes.*)

PSYCHIATRIST. And you'd been very . . . distressed about it? (KAY 1 *offers her cigarette.*) I don't thanks.

KAY 1. Do I have to answer these questions?

PSYCHIATRIST. Not if you don't want to.

KAY 1 (*lights up*). It was months ago. I was over it. I didn't talk about it 'cause it's not really relevant. Yeah, I was unhappy but you get on with things, you know?

PSYCHIATRIST. He's in Saudi now is he?

KAY 1 *nods.*

I suppose he might have heard about all this. It's been in most British papers hasn't it?

KAY 1. Every one printed. Fame at last.

PSYCHIATRIST. But you haven't heard from him?

KAY 1. No . . . (*Laughs.*) No. Why would I?

PSYCHIATRIST. Just a thought . . . (*Looks through papers.*)

KAY 1. I don't quite see what you're . . .

PSYCHIATRIST (*interrupts*). You used to go to that cottage a lot as a child didn't you?

KAY 1. Every year.

PSYCHIATRIST. What made you want to go back?

KAY 1. I just saw it in the book. It was dead cheap in March . . . (*Shrugs.*)

PSYCHIATRIST. Were you happy there, as a child?

KAY 1. Yes. We had some good times.

PSYCHIATRIST. But it wasn't the same going back?

KAY 1 *shakes her head.*

Had it changed?

KAY 1. No, the time, the time had changed.

PSYCHIATRIST. You never saw anything there before though?

KAY 1 (*wary*). How do you mean 'saw'?

PSYCHIATRIST. Any unusual . . . supernatural?

KAY 1. Why would I?

PSYCHIATRIST. Miss Douglas, when you were picked up you said you'd seen . . .

KAY 1 (*interrupts*). So? I was in shock.

PSYCHIATRIST. You've since talked to quite a few people, the nurses, your parents, Sheila, trying to describe what you . . .

KAY 1. Hallucinations due to hunger.

PSYCHIATRIST. You claimed they were genuine.

KAY 1. I've changed my mind.

PSYCHIATRIST. I see.

KAY 1. Did you read the papers?

PSYCHIATRIST. Some of them.

KAY 1. 'Something nasty in the woodshed. What did Kay Douglas, 24, see creeping round her lonely cottage in the wilds of Scotland?'

'Kay Douglas running battered and bleeding from her remote holiday home had been terrorised by the supernatural . . . ' usually followed by three paragraphs on poltergeists.

The whole of Britain now thinks either that I've been pursued through the woods by an assortment of wailing laundry or that I'm some kind of head case.

PSYCHIATRIST. And what do you think?

KAY 1. I think . . . I think I probably imagined things.

PSYCHIATRIST. Why would you do that?

KAY 1 *shrugs.*

Because you were worried about things? The job? The operation?

KAY 1. I wasn't worried about things! (*Quieter.*) I wasn't depressed or . . . anything like it.

PSYCHIATRIST. So why would you imagine things?

KAY 1 *shrugs.*

Don't you have an explanation?

KAY 1. There isn't any rational explanation.

PSYCHIATRIST. So you are saying you saw something supernatural?

KAY 1. I'm not saying anything any more.

PSYCHIATRIST. I see.

KAY 1. Well what do you think happened? Do you have an explanation?

PSYCHIATRIST. I think you may have imagined it, yes.

KAY 1 (*stares at her for a long moment, then quiet*). Why would I do that?

PSYCHIATRIST. You were overwrought, distressed . . . perhaps you'd been overdoing things.

KAY 1 (*under breath*). Putting in overtime on the franking machine, sure.

PSYCHIATRIST. Sorry?

KAY 1. Nothing.

PSYCHIATRIST. Or maybe you wanted to make some kind of gesture.

KAY 1. Don't follow.

PSYCHIATRIST. Ranks with attempted suicide in a way, breakdown . . . Maybe you I wanted to show this bloke in Saudi something? It's a possibility . . .

KAY 1. *What!?*

PSYCHIATRIST. We've got to consider every . . .

KAY 1 (*interrupts*). That's *ridiculous!*

PSYCHIATRIST. Is it?

KAY 1. What do you mean, 'Is it?' It's *crap!*

PSYCHIATRIST. Maybe I better leave you to rest now Kay.

KAY 1. Just who are you anyway?

PSYCHIATRIST (*pauses*). I'm a psychiatrist. I work here.

KAY 1. Who said you could come and talk to me?

PSYCHIATRIST. I had the permission of the consultant, and your parents.

KAY 1. What about me? What if I don't want you to?

PSYCHIATRIST. Everyone just wants to get to the bottom of this Kay.

KAY 1. What's to discover? I imagined it all. Everyone agrees on that don't they?

PSYCHIATRIST. I'll come back later. (*Walks forward to position during opening speech.*)

KAY 1 (*face screws up in sudden distress*). Oh shit. Why can't you all just leave me alone?

   KAY 2 *wanders on. She is wearing the same battered dressing-gown as* KAY 1 *in previous set. Her feet are bandaged. She watches* PSYCHIATRIST.

PSYCHIATRIST. It was always the same. Looking up under her fringe, a dark wary look, mouth sealing itself thinner and tighter . . . I was the enemy, the thing that was imprisoning her in this bare white room and forcing her to stare at herself too intently . . . Slipping out answers sideways, grudgingly letting them escape past her teeth . . . I think she was ashamed. 'A breakdown? Me?' I couldn't emphasise how common-place they were either. I think that made it worse . . . she wanted a wilder more exclusive kind of madness, she could live with that better. And yet . . . it didn't fit. I'd read her 'confessions' to the press, retold and rehashed a dozen times . . . there was something strange about them, something that nagged at me. She never actually said what she'd seen . . . She would give me this look, a blank wary stare, like something glaring out through bars with undefeated hatred. I kept up the brisk professional manner, but inside . . . I shivered.

I don't think I really thought she was upset about the job, the operation . . . I don't know what I thought . . . still don't . . .

KAY 2. It was real.

KAY 1 (*without looking up from cards*). Shut up.

KAY 2. I felt it.

PSYCHIATRIST. She was *terrified!* And her fear, because it seemed to have no source . . . frightened me.

KAY 1 (*to* PSYCHIATRIST). So you're a psychiatrist?

PSYCHIATRIST (*front*). That's right.

KAY 1. Aren't you a bit young?

PSYCHIATRIST. I'm still learning.

KAY 1. And you're practising on me?

PSYCHIATRIST. No. I know what I'm doing.

KAY 1. Why do you want to talk to me?

PSYCHIATRIST (*turns*). I thought it might be helpful.

KAY 1. Who for?

PSYCHIATRIST. Both of us.

Pause.

KAY 1. What's your name?

PSYCHIATRIST (*smiles*). Kay, Kay Nichols.

KAY 1. Coincidence.

PSYCHIATRIST. Mine's short for Katherine.

Pause.

KAY 1. I fancied being a shrink once.

PSYCHIATRIST. Why didn't you?

KAY 1 (*shrugs*). Didn't get the chance. Thought all you had to do was want to be something. Hadn't reckoned on exams.

PSYCHIATRIST. About your job, what exactly is it you don't like about it?

KAY 1. Here we go. I've *told* you.

PSYCHIATRIST *waits*.

Look it's just . . . *dull*, you know, monotonous.

PSYCHIATRIST. Isn't it the job you wanted?

KAY 2 (*quiet*). Type letters, file letters, make coffee . . . (*Continues to repeat this in quiet chant under subsequent dialogue.*)

KAY 1. It's a job.

PSYCHIATRIST. Why did you take it?

KAY 1. It was offered. There's a recession on you know . . . (*Stops herself.*) Sorry.

PSYCHIATRIST. But you thought you'd get something better?

KAY 1. Like your job for instance?

PSYCHIATRIST *waits again*.

I'd like something more interesting that's all.

KAY 2. Another eight hours, another pebble on the beach, unchanging, undramatic. The seconds of my life trickling down the plughole . . .

KAY 1. I could think of things I'd rather do with my time.

KAY 2 . . . . precious as blood.

KAY 1. How do you get to be a psychiatrist?

PSYCHIATRIST (*without turning*). I took a medical degree, then I specialised.

KAY 1. So what age are you? 25? 26?

PSYCHIATRIST. 25.

KAY 1. Did you take your exams early or what?

PSYCHIATRIST. I'm still studying.

KAY 1. Are you good at it?

PSYCHIATRIST. I hope so . . . (*Speaking front again.*) . . . same eyes, same age, same name . . .

Sorry Kay, suppose I'm just lucky.

All through subsequent action KAY 1 fiddles incessantly with cards. KAY 2 stands motionless turning a blank stare from one to the other.

PSYCHIATRIST. She was my first solo case. Before that it had been so easy, school, exams: endless pens dancing over endless blank sheets to the accompaniment of approving ticks in the margin. It was all a wonderful game with just enough challenge to give easy win after easy win a real sparkle. I've always run at things early, jumped fences I wasn't grown for. I used to think I was going to be a child prodigy once . . . well I grew up, so I blew that one . . . but fully qualified and practising psychiatry at 25? Oh that's a triumph, that's a real lie awake, count your blessings and smirk in nauseating self congratulation that one. I was a success story . . . That's what made all this such a shock, the amazement, the horrified amazement I felt looking at this unexpected body lying across my path, glaring balefully at me waiting to bite my feet when I tried to jump over her . . .

I didn't know what was wrong with her. I didn't know how to begin. At first I thought she was a bit of a fake, a melo-drama addict. The way she sat, held her head, everything screamed . . . 'I have been through a terrible ordeal, I've touched life at its raw core, gazed on demons and now I suffer for it.' (*Hand on brow.*) but then . . . I saw that under neath the prickles she was *so* scared and she was trying to hide it . . . that's what this dumb with suffering bit was all about. She was trying to play it down.

Then I thought: Maybe I'll botch this. Maybe in the glare of a thousand flashbulbs poised to capture my learned and precocious conclusions for the nation's press, I'm going to fall flat on my face. And for the first time in my life I really believed that *I* could fail. Not as an idea that gave the edge to some heady gambling with life but as a *fact*. I wasn't in control. *I* was terrified.

All that came out were the stiff formal catch phrases,
copybook questions that built a wall between us.

KAY 1. Why do you want to know about my dreams? I've told
you all this already.

PSYCHIATRIST *does not turn.*

KAY 1 (*sighs*). I saw a figure, a woman, sitting on the bed,
stopping me putting on the light . . . that sort of thing.

PSYCHIATRIST (*turns*). How did that make you feel?

KAY 1. I was scared. Couldn't even doze off, dreamt it again.

PSYCHIATRIST. So you stopped sleeping?

KAY 1 *nods.*

Go on.

KAY 1. Well then I just sat. Like I couldn't move. I was afraid
to move.

PSYCHIATRIST. Why?

KAY 1. I don't know. I felt something . . . terrible . . . was just
about to happen. Everything looked . . . wrong, like in a
nightmare you know? It's all familiar but it's *wrong* . . .
frightening . . .

Well that's it. I ran away . . .

PSYCHIATRIST. Nothing else happened?

KAY 1 (*pause*). No.

PSYCHIATRIST. You said something about a figure walking?

KAY 1. Oh yeah, that was the first day. I was up the hill and I
saw this figure down below, sort of pacing the ground without moving . . . it . . . it looked like they vanished. (*Shrugs.*)

PSYCHIATRIST. Did that frighten you?

KAY 1. I wasn't sure what I'd seen.

PSYCHIATRIST. But you've seen things like that before?

KAY 1. What?

PSYCHIATRIST. A little Victorian lady, the figure of a man . . .

KAY 1 (*soft*). Damn you Sheila Thompson . . . Yes. All right.
Yes I see things.

PSYCHIATRIST. So what do you . . . ?

KAY 1 (*interrupts*). I see things! That's all. I I don't know why or how or what I feel about it. O.K.? (*Busies herself with cards again.*)

PSYCHIATRIST (*front*). Yes . . . I believe she saw some thing.

I had dreams too. They started the first night after Kay Douglas was admitted . . . a dream I'd had before . . . There's a track you can see from the top of the hill at Glenbuchat, a minor road with grass down its middle. It's lined with trees. I dream I'm dying and as I'm dying I move further and further along this road, my feet nearly silent on the worn overgrown tarmac, a gentle green sunlight filtering down through the leaves . . . I know at the other end of the road is something that will swallow me up, but I'm not afraid. I try, but I can't *be* afraid . . . just the soft light, the soft footsteps, the quiet sound of the leaves overhead . . . and a walk that stretches further with each step I take . . . as though I were treading the road backwards under my feet but never moving . . .

The first night I saw Kay I dreamt that twice . . . after that it filled my sleep. Every time I dozed off . . . I dreamt it again . . .

KAY 1 *is rapidly laying out another spread of cards.*

KAY 1 (*referring to cards*). It's something to do.

PSYCHIATRIST. The *cards*. Why did she spend every second juggling that pack of cards?

Flicking and fluttering them around her bandaged fingers like a crippled conjurer.

KAY 1. It passes the time.

PSYCHIATRIST. Making them leap over each other like little paper acrobats then bringing them all to rest again.

KAY 1. I tell my fortune. Read my future in the cards, that sort of stuff.

PSYCHIATRIST (*turns*). Do you think it works?

KAY 1. Don't know. (*Shrugs.*) Sometimes.

PSYCHIATRIST. How would it?

KAY 1 (*looks at her, ' What are you driving at?'*). I don't
    know . . . It's like time's elastic, you know? It's free, it does
    what it likes, we're just carried along on the swell. (*With
    growing animation.*) Here's your past here, (*Indicates
    cards.*) the things that have happened to you, but you don't
    understand the implication of them, you've no way of telling
    what the *real* effect of even the smallest action is going to be
    . . . so the cards treat it like an equation you see, there's what
    you've done (*Points.*) and here's the possible outcomes . . .
    the future you can never predict . . .

PSYCHIATRIST: So you believe everything's predetermined?

KAY 1. No, no, we make our own futures, but blind, like
    slipping on banana peel, we're never in control, we can't see
    what the end result of our actions will be, we just line up and
    wait for the unexpected to knock us sideways . . .

PSYCHIATRIST. What's that card mean then?

KAY 1. The Queen of Spades? In that position it means
    someone who's going to have a profound effect on my
    future, woman, perceptive, good at managing people . . .
    reversed like that . . . (*Pauses then quotes from memory.*) A
    thoroughly evil woman whose attractive exterior conceals
    hatred, cruelty, treachery, malice and deceit . . .

Pause.

KAY 1. Do you think life works out for the best?

PSYCHIATRIST. I don't know. Sometimes.

KAY 1. How about history? Does that work out for the best?

PSYCHIATRIST. Depends what you mean.

KAY 1. Nothing we can do about it either way I suppose.

PSYCHIATRIST. I suppose not. What's your future then?

KAY 1 (*quiet*). It isn't there. I do spread after spread . . .
    Nothing. (*Stares up at* PSYCHIATRIST.)

PSYCHIATRIST (*nervous laugh*). So it doesn't always work
    then?

KAY 1 *says nothing.*

Kay? Why did you ask who I was, that first day I talked to you? You'd seen me before that, the first night you were admitted.

KAY 1. I don't remember.

PSYCHIATRIST. You saw Sheila and your parents the next day didn't you?

KAY 1. Yes.

PSYCHIATRIST. And that's when you told them about the dreams?

KAY 1. Yes. Why?

PSYCHIATRIST. No reason. (*No longer to* KAY 1.) I know she saw me. I *know*.

KAY 1. I don't remember seeing you.

PSYCHIATRIST. Well you'd been sedated. I looked in with the consultant for a moment that's all. (*No longer to* KAY 1.) They were struggling to keep her under the covers, she kept thrashing dopey limbs as if she was trying to keep walking. The consultant said 'Maybe you should give her another sedative' and she looked up at him then past him to me and she *froze* with that stare . . .

KAY 1 (*as if she has been racking her memory.*) I don't remember. Sorry.

PSYCHIATRIST. I better leave you to rest now. We can talk again tomorrow.

KAY 1. Won't I get home tomorrow?

PSYCHIATRIST. Perhaps.

KAY 1 (*looks down at cards*). I don't feel I ever will sometimes.

PSYCHIATRIST. Oh come on Kay, you've only been here a couple of days! It can't be as bad as all that.

KAY 1 *just stares at her.*

Well . . . I'll see you tomorrow.

KAY 1 *nods.* PSYCHIATRIST *walks away from her forwards.* KAY 2 *now wanders to stand between them.*

KAY 1. I don't think she believes in me. She thinks I faked it all.

KAY 2 (*insistently*). I see things.

PSYCHIATRIST. I don't understand her.

KAY 1. She thinks I'm spoiled, that I'm throwing a tantrum because I haven't got a cushy job like hers . . . because life didn't turn out the way I always felt it would . . .

KAY 2: Dropped me in my cot and talked me to sleep with stories about rabbits . . .

PSYCHIATRIST. I think I upset her . . .

KAY 1. I'd've liked a job like hers . . .

KAY 2. Take my exams and travel the world . . .

KAY 1. *Did* I fake it all?

KAY 2. Something out of the dark, scenting me, hunting me . . . warning breath on my neck.

PSYCHIATRIST. What could she have seen there anyway?

KAY 2. Always summer. The sun licking your flesh like a hot tongue . . .

KAY 1. That place . . . it's beautiful.

KAY 2. The air was full, mist in the morning, dancing midges in the evening . . .

PSYCHIATRIST. I don't understand. I don't understand what's wrong with her.

KAY 1. What's *wrong* with me?

KAY 2. Seeds of death inside me . . . the unexpected, thundering out of the future like a juggernaut.

PSYCHIATRIST. If it was just stress, some man, her job, why would she frighten *me*?

KAY 2. I'm not in control.

KAY 1. This feeling . . . something terrible's just about to happen.

KAY 2. I'm not in control.

KAY 1. I won't be afraid. I won't! (*Pause.*)

PSYCHIATRIST. If I could just once have broken through the barbed wire and *touched* her. Whatever it was that terrified her, it *can't* have been anything we couldn't have helped her with . . . (*Speaking to* KAY 2.) Oh Kay.

KAY 2. Nothing. Nothing at all.

Light fades.

PSYCHIATRIST (*quiet*). Kay.

Darkness.

The PSYCHIATRIST *now speaks with dead flat voice of the* GHOST.

GHOST. Kay.

KAY 1. Put the light on Kay, reach out, that's it, come on, come on!

GHOST. Hungry.

KAY 1. Oh no. Oh please don't.

GHOST. Hungry.

KAY 1. Don't, DON'T!

GHOST. Kay.

KAY 1 *screams. The light goes on. The* PSYCHIATRIST *is sitting on the bed holding* KAY 1'*s shoulder with one hand and the light switch with the other.*

PSYCHIATRIST. Kay. Wake up, Kay!

KAY 1. Oh Jesus.

PSYCHIATRIST. You were having a dream. It's all right now. It's over. It's all right.

KAY 1. I thought . . . it was there again . . . I thought . . .

PSYCHIATRIST. It's O.K.

KAY 1. Have you got a hanky?

(PSYCHIATRIST *hands her one.*) Thanks. (*Blows her nose.*) Thank you.

PSYCHIATRIST. Was it the same dream?

KAY 1. Mmmm.

PSYCHIATRIST. Do you want something to help you sleep?

KAY 1 *nods.* PSYCHIATRIST *gets her a sleeping pill.*

KAY 1. Putting in overtime?

PSYCHIATRIST: I was just working late on some notes.

KAY 1. Am I that fascinating?

PSYCHIATRIST *smiles and hands her a pill.*

I'm sorry. I was so scared. I'm sorry.

PSYCHIATRIST. That's O.K.

KAY 1. I don't understand it . . . I don't know what it is . . . I'm not faking all this you know.

PSYCHIATRIST. I know.

KAY 1. I thought you didn't believe me.

PSYCHIATRIST. I don't think I did at first . . . (*Hesitates.*) No, you're not faking.

Slowly they grin at each other.

Take your pill now.

KAY 1. What is it then? What's wrong with me?

PSYCHIATRIST. You've just had a minor breakdown, that's all, you're going to be all right.

KAY 1 (*studies her for a moment*). You know you asked me about seeing you that first night? I did see you. I remembered. But . . . it scared me . . .

PSYCHIATRIST. Why?

KAY 1. I recognised you. But I don't remember seeing you before. Ever.

PSYCHIATRIST. You weren't in the most rational frame of mind you know.

KAY 1. I'm afraid. I'm so afraid.

PSYCHIATRIST. Why Kay? What is it?

KAY 1 (*almost to herself*). Fate. Chance. A blind, brute force that sits in me and everyone and gambles our tiny lives, second by second . . . a blind brute force . . . I'm not different you know, there's nothing special about me, none of us are in control . . . but *I* . . . *see* things . . .

PSYCHIATRIST (*gentle*). I don't understand Kay. What do you see?

KAY 1 *hesitates*.

What did you see at . . .

KAY 1 (*interrupts*). I want to tell you. (*Stops, biting her lip.*)

PSYCHIATRIST. Take your pill.

She swallows it obediently.

You can tell me tomorrow.

KAY 1. I will. I'll tell you everything . . .

PSYCHIATRIST. Tomorrow.

KAY 1. I'll tell you tomorrow.

PSYCHIATRIST. Try and get some sleep now. (*Moves to exit, pauses.*) Goodnight.

KAY 1 *stares forward blankly. She doesn't respond.*
PSYCHIATRIST *exits. Lights fade.*

Scene Two

Lights up on KAY 1, *in spot she was in at start Act One.* KAY 2 *is seated in the chair exactly as she was at end of Act One.*

KAY 1. I couldn't move. Something terrible was just about to happen. I was *waiting* like a mouse watching for the movement of a paw outside its hole . . . a rabbit crouched in the road with headlamps in its eyes . . . I couldn't escape . . .

Very faintly the sound of someone singing 'Queen Mary' is heard, then on top of it KAY 2 *also on soundtrack, whispering:*

Type letters, file letters.
I'm going to be a rock star, a rally driver,
A hot mouth, a great hot mouth.

What difference does it make? What difference does it make?
Endless pens dancing over endless blank sheets.
Easy win after easy win.
Twisted limbs and scorched cooked skin . . .
I can fail. I can fail . . .

All phrases whispered in a chant, muttered and repeated,
overlapping with each other, as the volume builds up the
same phrases are played backwards on the soundtrack
adding chaos to the repeated murmur. The volume surges up
and down in a feverish mass of sound.

KAY 2 *looks round at* KAY 1*; they stare at each other for a*
few seconds then KAY 2 *rises and offers her seat.* KAY 1
walks over and seats herself. KAY 2 *remains standing at*
the back of the chair.

The PSYCHIATRIST *enters. She stares at* KAY 1*. Her lips*
form the words, 'Kay? What is it? Kay?' But she is not
audible above the mess of noises. She starts to walk towards
KAY 1*. As she does so the light goes down until only the*
two KAY*s are lit. The* PSYCHIATRIST *vanishes into the*
shadows. The noise reaches a crescendo then cuts out.

KAY 1 (*stirs*). Why is it so dark?

KAY 2 (*hesitating, distressed*). When I was two . . . my father . . .
he talked me to sleep with a bedtime story . . . He talked
away the dark.

KAY 1 . . . . and I fell asleep, safe in the shadows and his
voice . . .

KAY 1. Creeping through the wood, I was a *tiger . . . a*
hunter . . . Running . . .

KAY 2 (*trying to force the words out*). And I saw, I saw . . .

KAY 1. A rabbit.

KAY 2. It had no head. Oh *Mum*! It had no head !

KAY 1. And I ran, hunted, to escape what ate the rabbit . . . not
the fox or cat, but the force that moved their killing jaws and
fed their hunger . . .

KAY 2 (*frantic*). And it could eat me . . . It could!

KAY 1. When I was twenty-four . . . (*Stops, shaking, tries again.*) . . . When I was twenty-four I went back . . . to the cottage . . . (*Starts to get up.*)

KAY 2 (*telling a kids' story*). Kay went to a little house and Kay sat in a big armchair, all alone, in the dark, and Kay saw . . . she saw . . .

The GHOST *starts to move into* KAY 1*'s light.*

KAY 2 (*quiet at first growing rapidly louder*). Run Kay, run Kay, run Kay, run Kay. RUN!

KAY 1 (*yells in terror, each word distinct*). I don't want to die!

The GHOST *grabs her from behind . * KAY 1 *screams. Blackout.*

KAY 2 (*singing in darkness*).
Queen Mary, Queen Mary, my age is sixteen.
My faither's a fermer on yonder green,
He's plenty o' money tae dress me sae braw
But there' s nae bonny laddie will tak me awa.

Lights up. The PSYCHIATRIST *is alone on stage. She cradles her arms as if still holding* KAY 1.

PSYCHIATRIST. It wasn't my fault. It *wasn't*. It was an accident. You have to believe me, it was an *accident!* (*Slowly lowers her arms, gets herself under control again.*)

Shock. Her heart just . . . stopped. I don't know why, if I knew that . . . (*Stops herself.*) It was an accident. It was the end of a long line of accidents. I revolve them round and round in my head. If I hadn't been on the case, if she hadn't been in such a state, if neither of us had ever gone to that cottage . . . if I hadn't tried to touch her, break in on her terror . . .

It was an accident.

It all comes to the same thing, she's dead, what does 'why' matter?

It all comes to the same thing in the end.

What difference does it make?

What did she see? Me. Same age, same eyes, same name, same memories . . . different set of accidents. (*Shrugs.*) She saw things. Maybe that showed her something more. I don't know. I don't understand any of it. It changes everything. Maybe I'll change my job. I've got to get away by myself, sort things out. It changes everything. That's what I felt looking down at her surprised dead face, shock, not that something like this could happen at all but that it could happen to *me*. You never think it will do you?

I feel I want to move, change names, job, everything. All the people and places that were so comfortable and familiar suddenly look alike. Like something in a nightmare, as if she left me her way of looking at them sideways . . . I've got to move, to run, to *live* past this somehow, I *must* . . . but I don't see how. I've fallen over a cliff I didn't know was there. I can see Kay lying at the bottom . . . but I'm still falling.